ENTERPRISE CRIME

ENTERPRISE CRIME

Asian and Global Perspectives

Edited by Ann Lodl and Zhang Longguan
with an Introduction by Richard H. Ward

The Office of International Criminal Justice
with The Shanghai Bureau of Justice and
The East China Institute of Politics and Law

Library of Congress Cataloging-in-Publication Data

Enterprise crime : Asian and global perspectives / Richard H. Ward
[editor].
p. cm.
English and Chinese.
Includes bibliographical references and index.
ISBN 0-942511-60-3
1. Organized crime—China. 2. Organized crime—Prevention.
3. Narcotics and crime—China. 4. Narcotics, Control of. I. Ward,
Richard H.
HV6453.C6E58 1992
364. 1'06'0951—dc20

92-28793
CIP

CONTENTS

PART II

GLOBAL PERSPECTIVES

CONTRIBUTORS

Michael Ahern is an Assistant Inspector with the United States Postal Inspector Service.

Cai Cheng is the Minister of Justice of China.

Mark S. Gaylord is Senior Lecturer in Criminology at City Polytechnic of Hong Kong.

Julio Heredia is Social Affairs Officer of the Crime Prevention and Criminal Justice Branch, Centre for Social Development and Humanitarian Affairs at the United Nations in Vienna.

David Hodson is Chief of the Narcotics Bureau in the Royal Hong Kong Police.

Shi Huanzhang is President of the East China Institute of Politics and Law in Shanghai.

Edward James Kelly Jr. is Special Agent of the U.S. Drug Enforcement Administration in Hong Kong.

Edwin Kube is Director of the Research and Training Institute and Professor of Criminology at Giessen University in Wiesbaden.

Lai Bojin is associated with the People's Procuratorate of Shenzhen.

Liu Tongie is Director of the Research Center of the Shanghai Higher People's Court.

Frederick T. Martens is Executive Director of the Pennsylvania Crime Commission.

Qui Shigui is Deputy Chief Procurator of the Shanghai Municipal Procuratorate.

Joseph Serio is an International Representative of the Office of International Criminal Justice at the University of Illinois at Chicago.

Richard H. Ward is Vice Chancellor for Administration and Director of the Office of International Criminal Justice at the University of Illinois at Chicago.

Wu Han is Professor of criminology at the East China Institute of Politics and Law in Shanghai.

Xu QingZhang is Deputy Director of the Public Security Research Institute of the Public Security Ministry in Shanghai.

Xue Mingren is Director of the Shanghai Bureau of Justice.

Yuan Yougen is a member of the Shanghai Criminology Society.

Introduction

by Richard H. Ward

Enterprise crime involves local and regional problems that now extend into the international arena. Two or three individuals, committing sporadic capers, increasingly become woven into global networks of highly organized crime involving drug trafficking, the exporting of goods, and the sale of people. Consequently, the enmeshment of youthful hooliganism and mafioso presents new problems for law enforcement officials.

In the summer of 1991, the Office of International Criminal Justice at the University of Illinois at Chicago, in association with the East China Institute of Politics and Law, conducted a symposium to explore trends in enterprise crime. Participants from seven countries and numerous organizations took part in this conference. These papers from international researchers and practitioners provide a wide range of concerns, and each strives to provide an overall picture for future strategies. Usually conference contributions treat justice-related issues, social relations, ideology and politics as peripheral; in *Enterprise Crime*—particularly the submissions from our Chinese colleagues—these different aspects of human experience are part of an interconnected whole.

The boundless aspects of enterprise crime encourage the need for justice-related groups in all countries to work together. *Enterprise Crime* particularly aims to acknowledge the communal interests between China and other countries.

Part One offers essays that explore the crucible of crime in China during the 1980s. Cai Cheng, representing the Ministry of Justice, offers an introduction to this historical concern and task. By defining China's historical assignment in the last decade of the twentieth century, Minister Cai acquaints the reader to China's major considerations and unobtrusively affords an overview to his country's approach to crime. An essay by Xu QingZhang analyzes enterprise crime and public order. Through an integrated approach, Mr. Xu explains patterns that evolved in China since the opening of China in 1979. The author's keen description of clique and group crime enables readers to understand China's evolving legal practices.

Five essays contributed by Xue Mingren, Qi Shiqui, Yuan Yougen, Lai Bojin, and Liu Tongie describe local and regional variations of organized crime and suggest measures for comprehensive treatment. Each paper provides insights into China's collective mobilization efforts, involving educational remedies and adjudicative measures used to prevent various types of enterprise crime. Because China actively enlists its citizenry in crime prevention, the authors contend that enterprise crime will not be given much of a chance to grow within its borders. Each writer specifically documents how China's concerted approach aids in eradicating enterprise crime. To the Western reader, their papers will be particularly noteworthy.

The following three essays presented by Shi Huanehang, Mark Gaylord, and David Hobson furnish broad perspectives by discussing drug trafficking and money laundering in Asia. Both Shi and Gaylord track China's drug problem over time—or lack of it during the middle decades of this century. Their historical portrayals adeptly provide background data which substantially confirm what law officials assumed: drug trafficking and money laundering schemes are not new problems. The fact remains that past experiences with the drug trade bulk large in assessing current events and forecasting future trends. Today's more global dimensions of these crimes, however, make law enforcement officials as well as the public take notice. Each author helpfully extends his thesis by weaving the past into contemporary concerns and by indicating ways to ameliorate criminal activities. Hobson lends his voice to Shi and Gaylord's position by competently delineating the types of drugs used in these criminal industries, and his situation report covers important legislation relative to Southeast Asian crime control.

Part Two expands upon the global impact of enterprise crime. Julio Heredia from Vienna's International Center describes the United Nations' role in crime prevention. His contribution provides some answers to the question of how, in terms not wholly inconsistent with global governance, can officials concerned with law enforcement deal with the injurious effects of China's open door policy. By describing the global work currently undertaken by Vienna's Crime Prevention and Criminal Justice Branch, Heredia suggests the need "to create an international penal order."

Wu Han examines the conceptual and practical differences between crime in China and the West and emphasizes China's social and political systems of government. Mr. Wu describes assorted views of crime and society gleaned from years of government service. His work provides a basis for another look at the question of how the reader might view the problems posed by enterprise crime. Bundeskriminalamt's leading researcher, Edwin Kube, suggests the need for qualitative theories and methodologies for addressing transnational crime. His essay offers both a vision and a road map, and it delineates a research project that has taken the lead in this direction.

Michael Ahern's work proffers yet another perspective which outlines the crime prevention mission of the United States Postal Inspection Service. This enforcement body has been honing its techniques for more than 200 years in efforts to curb violations of postal laws. Ahern, however, adds another dimension to his background data by explaining how the inspection service has entered upon international mail investigations and furnishes the reader with inspection service remedies for postal crime.

The offerings of Frederick T. Martens, Executive Director of Pennsylvania's Crime Commission, and Edward J. Kelly, Jr., a special agent working in Hong Kong, craft their themes around authorizing group efforts. Martens concentrates on the invaluable service of crime commissions, and Kelly focuses upon the increasing success from cooperative efforts among drug enforcement agencies working in Southeast Asia. These two viewpoints vividly illustrate how a country's internal and external projects foster public education and assist in crime prevention.

The final selection by the Sovietologist, Joseph Serio, was based on a nine-month internship at the Sixth Department for Organized Crime Control under the auspices of the Ministry of Internal Affairs. Serio skillfully examines organized crime in the Soviet Union prior to the August, 1991 failed coup. His prescient comments about the problems then facing the Ministry and their effect on the international community will challenge law enforcement agencies throughout the Commonwealth of Independent States.

By examining all these global and regional patterns, we can better understand the impact of enterprise crime on individuals and societies and how our law enforcement community continuously strives to overcome these conditions. No one would deny we live in changing times, and the politics in each country serve as the public expression of the private needs and values of the social order. These facts remain apparent to all of us who have dedicated our lives to justice-related activities and who have recognized the immediate need to share our knowledge in creating a better world. Enterprise crime, by concocting both a complex process and an intrusive environment, often thwarts our energies. However, we all stand to benefit enormously, it seems to me, by consolidating our research and understanding in fighting crime on an international level.

In conclusion some words of thanks are due. The Office of International Criminal Justice (OICJ) supported this work, and remains steadfast to the advancement of humane justice systems throughout the world. Members of the Public Security Research Institute of the Public Security Ministry, Shanghai's Criminology Society, Shenzhen's People's Procuratorate, and the Federal Office of Criminal Police, Wiesbaden, FRG, among others, gave not only their consent to this project but also their valuable advice. These organizations and the labors of the contributors enhance the cause of comprehending the manifold aspects of enterprise crime. The staff of OICJ wishes to thank Professor Zhang Longguan for his meticulous comparisons of the original Chinese contributions, the English translations by the Chinese, and the edited versions of the contributions in English. Lastly, this work was completed with the help of Erika Maybon's computer skills and Bernadette Oden's production design. Experience and technical expertise contribute to our daily endeavors with international efforts and strategies and support our mutual walk into the twenty-first century.

Note

To readers of the Chinese contributions to this volume, two matters may need some clarification. The expression—comprehensive treatment to social order—can best be understood as an abbreviation of comprehensive treatment (of the whole society) to (achieve the national goal of) social order.

In the early 1990s, the exchange rate for one yuan was approximately $0.25 and for one Hong Kong dollar was approximately $0.14.

PART I

ASIAN PERSPECTIVES

An Introduction to China's Legal and Social Systems

by Cai Cheng

The historical task of the Chinese government and Chinese people for a comparative long time into the future is to concentrate efforts on the socialist modernization and on the development of domestic economy, so that the GNP of 1980 will be quadrupled by the end of this century and the people's living standards will be raised from being sufficient in food and clothing to a comfortable life. Internationally, China follows the peaceful diplomatic policy of independence and initiative, continuously expanding exchanges and sincere cooperation with various countries of the world on the basis of the Five Principles of Peaceful Co-existence. The Fourth Plenary Session of the Seventh National People's Congress adopted the "Ten-year Program and the Eighth Five-year Plan for National Economic and Social Development of the People's Republic of China" which have drawn a grand blueprint for the overall political, economic and social development and progress of China. In the coming ten years, while continuing to persist in reform and to open the nation further to the outside world, China, centering around economic construction, will do its utmost to strengthen its socialist democracy and socialist legal systems. The Chinese government has attached great importance to the construction of a legal system based upon principles: "there are laws to be followed; laws must be followed; be strict in the enforcement of law; violations of law must be prosecuted." Since 1979, China has made great progress in the construction of its socialist legal system.

In legislation, from 1979 to the present, the National People's Congress and its Standing Committee has promulgated 103 laws including the Constitution. The State Council has enacted 500 administrative laws and regulations. The congresses and their standing committees at provincial levels have adopted 2,000 local laws and regulations. The basic laws concerning civil, criminal, state structural and administrative matters have now generally been formulated. Economic laws have been or are being perfected. China's socialist legal system, based on the Constitution, has been preliminarily established, and laws exist on the basic and main aspects of China's political, economic, and social life. Consequently, democratic rights of the people as masters of the country can be guaranteed, and the economic development and social stability can be ensured.

In the field of justice since 1979, China has resumed and perfected the judicial agencies composed of the people's courts, people's procuratorates, and judicial administrative agencies. From the central government to localities, judicial institutions have been established and judicial ranks have been reinforced, and their work procedures and systems improved. The judicial agencies have adhered to the principles:

"independent trial of cases" and "everybody being equal before the law". The principle— "to rule the country by law"—has resulted in Party organizations and governments at various levels functioning within the limits of the Constitution and other laws.

China has a reestablished legal profession, notary public offices, and the people's mediation system. By 1990, there were more than 3,600 law firms in the entire country, with 50,000 lawyers and other people handling four million criminal, civil, economic, or other kinds of cases a year. China has 2,900 notary public offices with 15,000 personnel issuing six million certificates a year. Approximately 1.02 million mediation committees have been established with over six million members mediating more than seven million civil disputes each year.

In administrative law enforcement, since 1979, China has reestablished or has newly established a large number of administrative law enforcement agencies that oversee customs, taxes, industry and commerce, environmental protection, quarantines, and land administration. These institutions at all levels have been strengthened, their ranks enlarged, their work procedures and systems established. Especially, administrative litigation and an administrative review system have also been established. Citizens can sue government officials for their violations of law or of discipline before courts in administrative cases. Large numbers of administrative cases are filed with the courts every year. These court cases guarantee that governments at various levels will do their work in a legal way. Due to the continuous strengthening of the legal system and the continuous improvement of judicial and law enforcement work, China's political, economic, and social stability has been guaranteed with the socialist democratic politics and economic construction developed.

Comprehensive treatment to the social order is a correct policy for solving social order problems. It has been advocated by the Chinese government on the basis of historical experience. Generally the social order in China is good, but, with the expanding and deepening of reform and with the development of a commodity economy, some new problems have been brought to the social order. Most striking are the criminal activities such as theft, robbery, corruption, smuggling, and profiteering with unjust means done by some people who, seeing the fast increase of social wealth, blindly and greedily seek excessive material consumption and a high standard of living. In recent years, those criminal activities have increased. Meanwhile, enterprise crimes have also started to become obvious. When dealing with such social order problems, China, proceeding from its own national conditions, adheres to the principle of combining the specialized institutions with the efforts of the masses. Under the leadership of the governments at various levels, all resources of the society are mobilized and coordinated and involve all units and departments. To apply comprehensive treatment to social order, political, economic, administrative, cultural, and educational measures are used. China has achieved outstanding results. To practice comprehensive treatment to social order, judicial agencies and legal workers publicize the law on a broad scale and in depth to, strengthen the citizens' legal consciousness and the concept of observing law. They also stress their voluntary role in fighting against crime to create a sound legal environment of social order and to prevent and decrease the occurrences of crimes.

Essential to comprehensive treatment is intensified education. It is basically a strategical measure, especially in enhancing law-publicity work among young people and promoting their concept of the legal system. In 1986, China began its first five-year law publicity program among all citizens. Judicial agencies and publicity departments of Party committees, cooperating with each other and centering on the essential work of the period, did extensive publicity work on the Constitution and other laws under the leadership and supervision of Party committees, People's Congresses, and governments at various levels. The first five-year law-publicity program was completed in 1990, and good results were achieved. Among the 750 million who need such education, more than 700 million have studied ten laws including the Constitutional, Criminal Law, and Civil Law. Law courses are taught to students in all universities, middle schools, and specialized colleges. In primary schools, courses on morality are taken by pupils for the cultivation of their legal consciousness. Through law-publicity work, all officials and the masses have grasped to different degrees some basic knowledge of law. Education has strengthened citizens' consciousness of law, enhanced their voluntariness to fight against crimes, maintained a situation of unity and stability, and promoted the work of comprehensive treatment to social order. China's law-publicity work continues and the second five-year program on law-publicity began again in 1991.

Judicial agencies and legal workers also crack down resolutely on all crimes, especially on those with the characteristics of enterprise crime. Public security agencies are concentrating their forces to investigate and solve criminal cases. They concentrate their efforts to attack crimes that have been committed frequently and to capture a number of serious criminals promptly. Procuratorates and courts coordinate their work in prosecuting and trying cases without delay. China reacts immediately to criminal gangs wherever they make their first appearance to prevent their expansion. If these gangs are not stopped, the results will be more disasterous; they will form a degenerate force to tyrannize certain areas. Consequently, China has a policy of "capturing all gang members at one stroke" to prevent the emergence of mafia-like gangs. Since June 1990, after 250 days of intense work, the judicial agencies of Harbin, in Heilongjiang province, captured sixty-eight members, 62 of whom were prosecuted or sentenced. They also seized thirty-eight weapons and stolen goods worth 1.5 million yuan. As a result, a number of swindles, thefts, and profiteering cases were solved, and social order was effectively maintained.

Legal workers and judicial agencies also strengthen the work of mediation to prevent and settle civil disputes and to avoid aggravating contradictions that lead to criminal cases. People's mediation is a legal system for settling civil disputes and for preventing the aggravation of contradictions. It is a good system of self-administration, self-education and self-service by the people. Through mediation, civil disputes can be resolved early so they do not become criminal cases, social contradictions can be moderated, and elements causing instability can be diminished. This work is a fundamental cure for the social order. The judicial administrative agencies are in charge of the mediation work. Due to the good leadership and administration by judicial administrative agencies at all levels, the mediation organizations have been developed quickly both in their ranks and in their professions. Since 1981, Chinese mediation organizations have mediated 71 million civil disputes, have prevented 780,000 disputes from becoming aggravated cases in which the life and property of the people may have been endangered, and have prevented 930,000 individuals from being injured or killed in those cases. They have effectively played their role as the first defense-line in the prevention of crime.

Judicial agencies and legal workers reform and educate inmates in prisons and reformatories, stabilize the order in correction institutions, raise the quality of reform, and decrease recidivism to stabilize social order.

In practicing comprehensive treatment to social order, stability of the order in prisons and reeduction-through-labor institutions, the improvement of quality of reform, and lowering of recidivism are very important. Reforming inmates is a special kind of preventive work through rehabilitation and education. To turn a great number of inmates into new law-abiding persons and to change negative factors into positive ones are most significant in maintaining a good social order.

We practice seriously a policy of "reform first, production second" in reform-through-labor work and a policy of "education, persuasion and redemption" in China's reeducation work. China always places emphasis on reform of imprisoned criminals and on education for administratively sentenced inmates. Recently, China has operated special schools in prisons or rehabilitation institutions, raising the inmates' cultural advantages through normal school education and enhancing their consciousness of law and morality through education on politics, literacy, ideology, morality, and on the legal system. As a result, their thinking can be changed, and their crimes can be confessed. Vocational and technical training is also extended to the inmates according to their own talents. They can learn certain trade skills which will help them return to society and commit no new crimes. In many places, agreements on education and help are made between the correctional institutions and the community concerned. They mobilize well-known individuals, experts, and professors to extend education and help to inmates. Former inmates are given appropriate jobs upon their release. All these measures have lowered the crime rate inside prisons and the escape rate annually, both rates reaching the lowest figure in historical record for several successive years. The repentance rate has increased yearly, while recidivism has been under ten percent. Consequently, the social order problems have been effectively prevented from reoccurring.

In carrying out their functions, lawyers and notary publics not only defend citizens' democratic and legitimate rights in a correct way according to law, but they also strive to be correct in determining the facts and application of law. Safeguarding respect of the law and protecting the citizens' legitimate rights are combined to enable the legal services to provide the comprehensive treatment to social order. Since 1981, Chinese lawyers have defended people in 1.59 million criminal cases and have guaranteed the quality of case trials. In these trials the citizens' lawful rights and interests have been protected, and various kinds of criminals have been steadily correctly and firmly sentenced.

Lawyers have also handled 450,000 non-litigious economic cases and represented in 50,000 economic litigations. As a result, economic disputes have been decreased and economic criminal activities combatted. Notary public offices have handled 26 million matters, among them, sixty percent are notarizations of economic contracts. In their practical work, notary public offices are strict in the application of law. They have resolutely restricted or exposed illegal acts and crimes in economic activities. From 1988 to 1989, Chinese notary public offices have prevented more than 20,000 violations of economic law, involving 24 billion yuan. Legal service institutions in towns and villages, centering on a general strategy of agricultural development, have also done a great deal of work to promote the stability of social order.

The Chinese government has attached great importance to the growth of the legal system and to the comprehensive treatment to social order. In the coming ten years with the Eighth Five-year Plan, China will further strengthen the authoritative role of the Constitution and the law on political, economic, cultural and social aspects or life. Certain laws and regulations will be made to address future needs and situations; effective laws and regulations will be carefully observed and enforced. China will further mobilize and will rely on the resources of society in practicing comprehensive treatment to social order to prevent and punish various kinds of offenses and crimes, to safeguard citizens' life, property, legitimate rights and interests, and protect the smooth progress in reform and opening to the outside world and in the socialist modernization drive.

Enterprise Crime and Public Order

by Xu QingZhang

Since the policies of reform and the opening to the outside world were accomplished in the late 1970s, China has made great progress in both economic construction and social development. The political situation remains steady, and social order and security are mainly good. However, some negative phenomena have emerged during the years of great, constructive transformation in concepts, economics, and social structures. The sharp increase of crimes, especially organized crime, is typical.

Organized crime is one kind of criminal activity that is most harmful to the social order and security. It has become one of the most serious and crucial problems in China. According to statistics from the investigation departments, organized crimes generally make up approximately one-third of all crimes, including theft, robbery, fraud, murder, assault, roguery, rape, smuggling, drug trafficking, and forgery.

Most groups committing such criminal activities are involved in theft, robbery, and fraud to gain possession of the state's and individuals' property. These organizations have caused the most serious damages to the society.

The organized crime in China is generally divided into two major types: One type is clique crime. These groups have ringleaders, usually a fixed membership, a clear division of labor, and a premeditated plan before committing crimes. To date, there is little clique crime in China.

The other type of organized crime in China is group crime, which has not entered the glossary in the country's current criminal code and law. The name has been created by the judicial and public security departments as they have been pursuing criminals who seriously endanger public security in recent years. Group crime generally refers to a group criminal activity which involves at least three individuals and which is often committed by criminals collectively and successively. Group crime is a primary form of organized crime. In it, many persons join together temporarily to commit crimes; the group is loosely structured; the membership is not steady. The members gather and disperse now and then, and their organization has no clear division of labor. Members of the group do not know each other's real names and addresses but only their nicknames or code names for one another. Group crime accounts for approximately ninety percent of all organized criminals in China.

The majority of the leaders of the criminal groups are habitual criminals or recidivists who, in opposition to and retaliation against the society, organize criminals and law-offenders into a group to commit crimes. Although these leaders generally comprise thirty percent of the total criminal group members, the criminal groups organized and manipulated by them account for more than sixty percent of all criminal groups. Although most career offenders and recidivists have been punished or penalized by public security or judicial departments, they have not changed their criminal habits; they still commit crimes. If chance permits, they gather together with other law-offenders and criminals or try to induce some young people to join their organization. These criminals act as the organizers and advisers in conducting criminal activities. Usually these recidivists possess a large criminal potentiality. They are well experienced in committing crimes and evading punishment. Undoubtedly, they are one of the main forces leading to the formation of organized criminal groups and resulting in rampant criminal activities.

Many crime group members are peasants; they account for sixty to seventy percent of crime group members. Most of them are poorly educated. More than eighty percent of the members of crime groups have only received an education below junior middle school levels. Most members are young people below twenty-five years of age, and they account for seventy to eighty percent of all crime group members.

Group crime seriously corrupts young people. It easily seduces young people who are unable to discriminate between right and wrong and who have little experience in society. Especially young people who have displayed some potentially criminal behaviors and have made mistakes are urged to join a group and commit crimes. According to the data from public security agencies on the structure of criminal groups of all kinds, juvenile delinquents have become the source personnel in crime groups. Juvenile delinquents represent 79.4 percent of the criminals among almost a thousand criminal groups apprehended in Hubei Province's Wuhan City in 1983. Among juvenile delinquents, those who participate in group crimes account for fifty-seven percent, with only forty-three percent left for non-grouping youths. Among those non-grouping juvenile delinquents were some who in fact belonged to a crime group but were counted as individual criminals, because they were captured when committing crimes alone. Of all criminal groups, young criminal groups account for 73.3 percent of them.

In 288 criminal group cases solved in the first half of 1986 in one city, 93.3 percent of the offenders were teenaged and young delinquents, of which 43.3 percent were below eighteen years of age. The proportion of juvenile and young grouping criminals is very large, and they have become the main forces in criminal groups in China.

The gathering of a criminal group is rather complicated. Many group crimes are committed by criminals temporarily and loosely associated. They gather according to region or clan, or they join together, because they come from the same town, the same clan, or they are colleagues, schoolmates, fellow workers, neighbors or friends. Generally they form a specialized group for thefts on railways, robberies on highways, or for drug trafficking. Most groups are comprehensive ones whose members gather together to conduct several kinds of criminal activities. Some of them commit illegal activities and commit crimes; some commit not only property crimes but also personal assaults; some not only assemble to fight, make trouble, and molest women, but also commit murder, rape, or gang rape; some not only commit ordinary crime but also conduct other criminal activities. Other groups dominate and control a certain region; others are constantly moving to commit crimes wherever they go.

China is a country with a long feudal history, and it once fell into a semifeudal and semicolonial society before the founding of the People's Republic of China. In the old China, every kind of secret society and organization existed in cities and in the countryside. Local ruffians, hooligans, stragglers, disbanded soldiers, bandits, local tyrants, gamblers, prostitutes, and gang-masters participated in a criminal force in the society of that time. These organizations had a very strong factional tendency, and there were rather strict rules and division of rights within the society. After the founding of the PRC, the government took very stern measures to ban and destroy secret societies, superstitious sects, and other reactionary secret societies and organizations. Severely punished were many vicious culprits and leaders; however, the thoughts of feudal secret societies are far from being eliminated. From an analysis of cases of criminal groups at present in China, the names, the inner structures, the types of activities, and the spiritual support such as oaths of personal loyalty of these groups are quite similar to those of the feudal societies and organizations in old China. In recent years, some criminal groups, especially juvenile crime groups, initiate and follow the ways of feudal societies and mafia organizations in gongfu (martial) and chivalrous stories and films which refer to kowtowing, smearing blood, swearing oaths as sworn brothers and sisters, arranging ranks, and making rules for the gang. They now call themselves the "Green Dragon Gang," the "Party of Beggars," and the "West Bank Moving Platoon." Their purpose is to condense and solidify the group itself, to show its power to intimidate and frighten others, and to dominate the local region. Most of the leaders in these crime groups consist of mostly young people, and as a result, the internal organizing structure of the group, its methods, and its purposes of committing crimes are imitative of well known mafia societies abroad.

Recently with the further implementations of reform and the open door policy, China has been absorbing and introducing advanced science, technology, and equipment from foreign countries. Some foreign criminal cliques and mafia societies take advantage of the occasion to permeate into the Chinese mainland through legal and illegal channels. They take the chance to collaborate with the law-offenders and criminal groups on the mainland to develop and expand their organizations. Since China is in transition from an old system to a new one and is developing a commodity economy, it is natural to lose control in some areas. Consequently, many group crimes are gradually developing into clique crimes, and some clustered gang crimes are growing into organized crimes. Criminal activities are increasingly becoming intellectualized and professionalized while the organized structure of the crime organizations daily becomes increasingly rigid. The mafia societies based in Hong Kong, Macao, and Taiwan develop and expand their organization to commit hooliganism, blackmail, theft, and robbery, especially in the coastal areas of China. In 1981, activities organized by secret societies based in Hong Kong were uncovered in Shenzhen. Frequently, some activities by outside secret societies such as the "14K," "Water House," "Sand Band," and "Bamboo Gang" were detected in the coastal regions in Southeast China. They have constantly expanded into some inland areas recently. China has already discovered some criminal activities committed by criminal groups at home together with secret criminal cliques abroad and outside of the border. In some boundary areas, criminals from China and abroad colluded to smuggle, traffick in narcotics, manufacture fake money for sale, and abduct people. In a case of trafficking which was uncovered by the public security agency in Fujian Province in 1989, the main gang members were from Taiwan-based secret societies. They sneaked onto the mainland and colluded with Chinese criminals to traffic and sell guns and pistols. The penetration and influence of outside secret societies has played a role in the development and the great increase of crimes in China. These organized crimes have attracted the attention of the Chinese government, and the public security agencies at all levels have considered the crackdown and prevention of organized crimes as one of the most important tasks in upholding stable social security and order.

To stop and prevent organized crimes, a policy of comprehensive treatment of social security must be followed. To keep a stable social secure order, to safeguard people's life and property, and to guarantee the reform, the open-door policy, and the course of the modernization of China, various effective measures have been adopted by the government and the public security departments at every level. These measures have reinforced the struggle against organized crimes.

China believes that if a nation wants to effectively stop and prevent organized crimes, it is necessary to enhance a comprehensive treatment of the security of the society. Organized crime is a special pathological, social phenomena, and the causes of its occurrence, development, and changes are multiple and complex. Organized crime is the central and comprehensive reflection of all the negative factors in Chinese society. Therefore, it will be a long-term and difficult job to strike at and prevent organized crimes, and it will not be enough to rely upon the efforts of the public security and judicial departments. China must rely on the efforts of all sectors of the society, adopt a policy to seek both permanent and temporary cures, coordinate the job of the public security and judicial departments with the masses, combine all political, economic, executive, educational, cultural, and judicial methods to prevent crimes and punish criminals, and confine and eliminate the conditions for the emergence of organized crime. Only in this way can organized crimes be reduced and restricted as much as possible; the steady social security and order of the country can be guaranteed, and the stability and development of the nation can be ensured.

The following are the concrete countermeasures taken in recent years by public security departments against organized crimes. First the departments have stopped organized crimes according to law. It has been stipulated explicitly in Chinese criminal law and criminal procedure law that the chief culprits of organized crimes be punished strictly and without delay so as to check the development of organized crimes. It clearly and elaborately stipulates in the 23rd, 24th, and 25th, articles of China's criminal law the principles of how to identify and treat the chief culprits in criminal groups. As stipulated in the 23rd article, individuals who organize and lead criminal groups to commit crimes or play a major role in a joint crime are major criminals, and as such, they must be given harsh punishments unless otherwise stipulated in specific provisions of this law. The law also makes it clear that the accessories and gang members who are coerced or trapped into committing group crime can be treated leniently or be exempted from punishment in order to disintegrate their crime group. In September 1983, the Standing Committee of the National People's Congress promulgated a decision on the severe punishment for criminals who seriously endanger the social order. It stipulates that a punishment, overpassing the harshest punishment fixed in the criminal law including the death sentence, may be inflicted upon the leaders of both the criminal hooligan groups and the groups who abduct and traffick in human beings. In judicial practice, China distinguishes between clique crime and group crime. Group crime is treated as joint crime. For clique crime, China relies on the principles of depending upon facts, hearing and trying the whole case, and severely punishing the leaders.

Second, public security departments enhance the fight against organized crimes in light of the features of organized crime which generally involves many people acting successively. In handling organized crime that crosses the borders of regions, the concerned regions and departments must coordinate action to put cases together for investigation. From the interrogating of captured criminals, investigators try to discover the origins of the organized crimes and track them down to uncover the crime completely. Investigators have severely cracked down on organized crimes and yielded good results. In 1983, the public security departments at all levels firmly acted upon the decision of the Standing Committee of the National People's Congress and resolutely, accurately, and forcefully attacked and destroyed many criminal groups, yielding a great result for the stability of China's social order. Presently in China, public security departments at all levels adhere to the policy of severely cracking down on all kinds of organized crimes and of destroying organized groups and severely punishing their leaders according to law. It is impossible for China to maintain a stable social order and security without linking the clearing of criminal cases with the severe crackdown on organized crimes and of adhering to a policy of firmly attacking crimes according to law. Third, public security departments link their professional work with the masses, build and perfect all security and prevention organizations, tighten social controls, pay close attention to the trends of organized crimes, and attack crimes as soon as they appear. For example, the masses are organized to patrol in cooperation with the police for a joint social defense. Presently, more than two million members belong to joint defense brigades in towns and in the countryside. The security and defense organizations in large factories, mines, and businesses have been strengthened; in towns and in the countryside more than 1.17 million public security committees in neighborhoods, and their more than twelve million members are playing roles to tighten social defense control. They have yielded positive results by discovering, controlling, striking, and preventing organized crime. In 1988, 35,985 criminals of all kinds were captured by the joint defense organizations in Beijing, Shanghai, and Tianjin. They also helped public security departments uncover 19,193 criminal cases.

Fourth, public security organizations enhance the collection and the investigation of information. Generally in organized crime, there is a period of planning and conspiring, and it involves many criminals. It is very important to be careful in collecting information. The main channels for public security departments to find and collect clues about organized crime are from individuals disengaged from criminal groups or criminal cliques, from interrogations of captured criminals, and from the investigations and clearances of criminal cases. Other sources for information include close association with the departments of public order, frontier guards, pre-interrogation, and security defense. The clues at hand must be inspected and verified quickly, and the criminal groups must be given a further investigation to verify evidence and make the whole case clear. As to those criminals who have not yet formed an organization, the most dangerous must be treated without delay so as to not allow them to form groups.

Fifth, public security organizations enhance the education of juveniles. The great increase in juvenile criminal groups is part of the problem of organized crime in China, and juveniles have become main factors in these kinds of crimes. Therefore, to prevent and lessen organized crimes, it is important to give juveniles untiring education in politics, ideology, morality, culture, and law to elevate their concept and consciousness of morality and law. Education will provide juveniles with knowledge of a citizen's basic rights and obligations, of the laws and disciplines relating to their lives and work, and of what is law-breaking and crime. Education will help them form good law-abiding habits, be conscious of themselves being subjected to socialist morality and law. They will learn how to use law as a weapon to defend their own legal rights and how to fight against crimes and safeguard the social order of their socialist country. Only with education can social contradictions be reduced, juvenile delinquency be diminished and prevented, and the purpose of the comprehensive treatment to social order and security be reached. To enhance the knowledge of law and the legal system, and to publicize the knowledge and consciousness of law of all people, the Standing Committee of the National People's Congress passed the "Decision on the Publicity of Knowledge of Law among Citizens" in November 1985. By the end of 1990, almost 700 million people in China had participated in the study of law. In March 1991, the Standing Committee passed the "Decision on the Further Development of the Education and Publicity of Law and the Legal System" to strengthen citizens' legal concepts and consciousness.

Because organized crime has been increasing and growing internationalized and secret societies from abroad have been penetrating the mainland, it will be very difficult to effectively attack those criminal forces without regional and international cooperation. The exchange and cooperation of police of different states and regions will be needed. The exchange of information should be enhanced among countries to inform each other of the new tendencies and characteristics of organized crimes so that they will learn the general trends of organized crimes. All countries should provide without delay other concerned countries and regions with information about multi-regional criminal organizations. These countries should try their best to make their investigations as soon as possible. Finally, the coordination of the headquarters of the international police should be brought into effect to coordinate the actions taken by every country in attacking transnational criminal organizations. If necessary, joint actions should be taken to attack organized crime more forcefully than has happened in the past.

Comprehensive Treatment to Social Order and the Prevention of Crimes

by Xue Mingren

Enterprise crime is the inevitable outcome when various criminal activities in a country or region have developed to a certain degree of seriousness. The degree of seriousness of a social criminal situation is an overall response to the social problems of security, i.e. various kinds of social contradictions and negative effects. In dealing with enterprise crime and criminal offenses, China must crack down on them strictly and promptly without any leniency. Nevertheless, to prevent criminal offenses is a systematic, social project. It requires the mobilization and coordination of the efforts of the whole society by implementing the policy of comprehensive treatment to social order and using political, legal, and educational measures. The Standing Committee of the National People's Congress of the People's Republic of China adopted the "Decision on Strengthening the Comprehensive Treatment to Social Order" on March 2, 1991. This Decision stipulates clearly the tasks, standards, and scope of the comprehensive treatment to social order.

Chinese justice administrative agencies are undertaking the responsibilities of administering and guiding the work, including publicity and education about the legal system, people's mediation, punishment, the reform of criminals, the legal profession, and notary publics. The agencies cover a broad range of society and work closely with the masses of the people.

In implementing the policy of comprehensive treatment to social order so as to thoroughly remove the social causes that generate enterprise crime, administrative agencies of justice enhance the legal and moral consciousness of citizens and cultivate everybody's concept of a voluntary fight against crimes by creating a comprehensive legal system.

Illegal acts and crimes are committed by people. It is possible to decrease illegal acts and crimes by helping citizens to distinguish legal acts from illegal ones, understand the rights and duties given to them, heighten their consciousness of self-help and self-restriction according to law, and use law as a weapon in the fight against illegal acts and crimes. Citizens learn through education about relevant laws, regulations, and decrees of the society. China has persisted in training people in law and has publicized the law as well. "The Resolution on the Publicity of Basic Knowledge of Law among Citizens," adopted at the Thirteenth Session of the Standing Committee of the Sixth National People's Congress in November 1985, specified that education should be extended to citizens about the Constitution, civil law, and other laws and regulations pertaining to the state structure of the country. By the end of 1990, approximately 700 million people had participated in the study of basic law in China. In

Shanghai, 7,572,000 people had received similar education. In 1991, the second nationwide five-year law-publicity program began. Administrative agencies of justice are in charge of law-publicity work and the publication and distribution of relevant magazines and study materials. Public security agencies, people's procuratorates, people's courts, and judicial agencies have established within their respective organizations law-publicity departments. In addition to lectures by experts, they have posted notices on walls in public places and made video tapes to publicize the law. The courts, in order to encourage people to become educated, announce sentences at public gatherings and print and distribute certain court judgments on large public posters. Recently, the Shanghai Municipal People's Procuratorate and the Shanghai Municipal Bureau of Justice have jointly held an exhibition of typical cases of corruption and bribery to enhance the vigilance of the whole people in resisting criminals and to fight against crimes. Crimes can be checked when law-publicity is combined with crackdowns, prevention, and administrative work to form a system of comprehensive treatment to social order.

Shanghai Yu Garden Street is a well known commercial and tourist center in the world. It also includes the old town of Shanghai with a population of 50,000 people in an area of 0.45 square kilometers. For many years because of the street committee's persistent law education and administrative work, the total criminal cases in 1990 decreased twelve percent compared to 1989; theft crimes decreased forty-three percent. During the fifteen-day celebration of National Day in 1990, the influx of people increased to 2.5 million, but not a single crime of misdemeanor occurred.

China has put special emphasis on intensifying law-publicity among young people. Young people growing up are natural targets of criminals. Recently, juvenile crime rates have been increasing. Among the criminals convicted and sentenced by the courts in Shanghai, juveniles comprised 42.3 percent of all offenders. In Shanghai City, a network has been established for the protection of juveniles at the levels of the municipality, the district or county, the street, and the neighborhood or village. Community Education Committees have been formed at the district and street levels. The administrative agencies of justice cooperate with other parts of society to do intensified law-publicity work among young people, establish law education programs for primary and middle schools, and compile textbooks of basic legal knowledge for them. Officers are frequently sent by the public security bureaus, people's procuratorates, people's courts, and judicial agencies to publicize the law in schools or act as spare time teachers working with the schools to help problem students amend their ways. Twenty-four lawyers now work especially on cases involving juveniles. These lawyers emphasize to the juveniles education in law and the observance of law to prevent them from becoming members of enterprise crime organizations.

With the aim of cracking down and preventing crimes effectively, different aspects of law-publicity are emphasized according to the practical situations during different periods and at different areas. In 1990 various kinds of publicity concentrated on specific crimes such as gambling, prostitution, pornography, and theft. With the development of the economy and the implementation of the policy of reform and a open marketplace, the influx of people has greatly increased, and some criminals committed crimes by taking advantage of these changes (among captured criminal offenders in Shanghai, approximately one-third were not residents of Shanghai). Therefore, intensified law-publicity was aimed at people from outside Shanghai. In the Baoshan District of Shanghai, there are 100,000 non-Shanghai residents with some criminals among them. Regulations on Strengthening the Administration of Non-Shanghai Residents were promulgated, and law-publicity work was included as an important component of intensified administration. Consequently, the social order in the Baoshan District was improved, and crime decreased. Shanghai County intensified the administration, publicity, and education to non-Shanghai residents and captured various criminal offenders, effectively checking the increasing crimes committed by non-Shanghai residents.

Recently, people have been increasingly involved in gambling, and thefts, robberies, and murders by gamblers were also increasing. In law-publicity, crimes associated with gambling were emphasized. North Shanxi Street in the Zhabel District used law-publicity as a weapon in combatting gambling, reducing the number of gamblers from 1,360 in 1988 to 125 in 1990, thereby limiting the social breeding grounds of criminal activities.

The establishment of residents' prevention organizations to strengthen the control of communities and forming an efficient line of defense for preventing crimes greatly help to stop criminals. At grass-root levels in China, several kinds of residents' prevention organizations cooperate closely and support each other. In Shanghai, security committees and mediation committees, with working forces of 350,000 and 110,000 respectively, are organized in neighborhoods, villages, towns, factories, mines, and business companies. The security committees assist in maintaining local social order, solving criminal cases, and arresting wanted, escaped criminals. The mediation committees mediate civil disputes among residents and help prevent crimes. In addition, other organizations exist such as the workers' pickets in business companies, united security brigades for maintaining social order, and residents' defense teams at neighborhood and village levels. Consequently, a strong army is formed to cooperate with specialized agencies in preventing, controlling, and dealing with crimes. Criminals are now under the watchfulness of millions of eyes; their space for criminal activities is diminished; their vicious crimes are effectively prevented.

Mediation committees comprise the first line of defense in the comprehensive treatment to social order. As the statistics of the Shanghai people's courts indicate, injury and murder cases arising from disputes in love affairs and marriages and between neighboring families comprise seventy percent of the total number of these two types of crimes. Many civil disputes may become crimes, if the contradictions in disputes are not resolved promptly and appropriately. As a result, the administrative agencies of justice regard the people's mediation as their major work. They appoint judicial assistants in government agencies at street and township levels and guide the mediation committees in settling civil disputes promptly and successfully. Their success has eradicated problems endangering the stability of the society and has prevented and reduced crimes.

The mediation work has drawn much attention from all of the society. The Shanghai Municipal Government once called a special meeting on the comprehensive treatment of civil disputes. Residents' mediation committees, public security agencies, people's courts, and women's federations cooperated with each other to improve the mediation network on the district or county, the street or township, and the neighborhood or village levels. Within large and medium-sized businesses, people's mediation committees have been established. Coordinated mediation organizations are established with the factory and locality concerned, and joint mediation organizations work in urban and countryside areas. Some combined mediation organizations were also formed by the counties of Shanghai and the neighboring cities and counties of other provinces. As a result, the areas with mediation services are enlarged; the vitality of mediation is strengthened; a resolution of social contradictions and civil disputes has been achieved.

When some former prisoners return to society after serving their sentences, they often encounter discrimination and a hostile reception. Conflicts between a former inmate and his wife or among family members may occur, and mediation committee members will come to mediate these conflicts, help former prisoners dispel their psychological problems, and try to solve their problems of unemployment. The members' help is very beneficial in the prevention of recidivism.

To turn criminals into reformed law-abiding people and to decrease the number of recidivists are more significant than the general fight against crimes. Chinese judicial agencies, in the course of setting criminal punishments, implement a policy of "reform first; production second." They integrate the reform work into the overall plan of comprehensive treatment to social order. They want to encourage former criminals to become laborers living on their own work, and they want to reduce recidivism.

The stability of correctional institutions is a prerequisite of good reform work and is also a way to prevent escape and recidivism. Various prisons and reformatories have adopted strict supervision, introduced standardized management, modernized the facilities and equipment, and taken strict precautions. The security and stability of correctional institutions have been maintained, and murder, escape, and other serious crimes have been prevented. The inmates' escape rate in Shanghai has decreased from 0.05 percent in 1987 to 0.02 percent in 1991.

In correctional work in Shanghai, the idea of educating and helping inmates is always kept in mind. Reform through education is combined with reform through labor, and strict administration is integrated with rehabilitation of inmates. Differing the management for major and minor criminals, stressing the cultural life to inmates, and providing special schools are all aimed at raising the rate of rehabilitation. Through labor, the inmates' habit of living on the labor of others can be cured. Certain kinds of skills can be learned, because trade education reaches seventy-seven percent of all inmates. Conditions have been created for the employment of inmates and for proper living after their return to society. Learning to read and write and to participate in recreational activities are helpful to the inmates in adjusting their spiritual life and reviving their feelings. In 1990, 7.26 percent of all inmates had their imprisonment shortened, while only 0.18 percent had their imprisonment increased.

In Shanghai's practical reform work, the resources of the whole society have been mobilized to turn negative effects into positive ones. When defending criminal cases, defense attorneys not only speak for the accused during court sessions, but they also explain the relevant laws and analyze the case to the accused and to family members. The government at all levels, the trade union, the youth league, the women's federation, democratic parties, juvenile protection organizations, the federation of individual businesses, and other governmental agencies and institutions of the society take their own initiatives in educating and helping inmates. Zhou Xiaolan, a former member of the Chinese women's volleyball team and a world champion, visited the Shanghai Municipal Prison to give talks to inmates on the purpose of life. Correctional institutions have invited the victims of crime to speak to the inmates to arouse their consciences. Inmates' family members are invited to attend seminars, and they are encouraged to persuade inmates to work on rehabilitation. Shanghai's Juvenile Reformatory has organized six seminars for inmates' parents in the Hongkou, Changning, and Xue Hui Districts of Shanghai, with an attendance of the parents of 230 juvenile offenders. Because recidivism would greatly endanger the society, the social care, the daily supervision, and education of inmates are important links in the comprehensive treatment to social order. Correctional institutions in Shanghai have concluded agreements to join in working with the district, county, and street administrations. In these agreements, revisits to former inmates by correctional personnel, education by the community, and assistance in finding jobs are mentioned specifically. A multi-tiered and many-sided network of help and education has resulted in great success. According to a survey of three successive years, the recidivism of 15,938 former inmates has decreased every year, declining from 10.9 percent in 1988 to 4.1 percent in 1990. China has, consequently, effectively prevented ex-prisoners from committing new crimes and has greatly weakened the social bases on which enterprise crime exists and develops.

Group and Joint Crime Distinctions in Law and Practice

by Qi Shigui

According to Articles 22 and 23 in Part I and related articles in Part II of the Criminal Law of The People's Republic of China, two kinds of joint crimes are legally defined: ordinary joint crimes and crime groups. Ordinary joint crime is meant under the Criminal Law to be intentional crime committed by two or more persons together. Crime group is a relatively stable crime organization created by a number of persons to commit certain crime or crimes over a comparatively long period of time.

In China's judicial practice, the term, gang crime, has constantly been employed to indicate a crime committed by three or more persons loosely grouped into some kind of organization. It is a new form of crime which falls between ordinary joint crime and group crime. The term, however, is not legal terminology; it is a descriptive characterization of a crime involving a team of a number of persons. Under the Criminal Law, such wordings as "gather a group," "assembled crowd," "mass(rebellion)" connote the essence of gang crime. China's practice is to treat gang crime as group crime if it has the basic features of a group crime, or as an ordinary joint crime if it bears no basic features of group crime. Currently, gang crimes are very prominent in various forms of crimes in China.

Joint Crime and Crime Group Legislation

Judiciary attention has centered on fighting group crime and gang crime and their leaders and principals—the main targets of law enforcement. During the twelve years after the promulgation of the Criminal Law, the judiciary has accumulated much experience in its fight against crime groups and gang crimes. Recognizing this experience, the legislature has increased its law-making, enacting a number of new statutes, including the "Decision on Sanctions against Escapees and Recidivists," the "Decision on Severer Punishment for Economic Crimes," "Decision on Severer Punishment for Criminals Gravely Endangering Social Peace and Order," an "Anti-Drug Decision," "Decision on Penalties for Smuggling, Making, Selling or Otherwise Disseminating Pornography," Supplementary Regulations against Smuggling, and Supplementary Regulations against Corruption and Bribery. The People's Supreme Court and the People's Supreme Procuratorate have given their judicial interpretations on the basis of judicial practice. These important Decisions and Supplementary Regulations and judicial interpretations provide in the Criminal Law specific and specialized remedies, thereby providing a more or less systematic set of criminal law norms governing crime groups and ordinary joint crimes.

The principle has been established for the severe punishment of ringleaders of crime groups or principals of ordinary joint crimes with aggravated circumstances. Under the Decisions and Supplementary Regulations either the maximum statutory penalties or penalties above the statutory maximum are provided for crime group leaders or leaders of ordinary joint crimes. Such grave economic crimes with extraordinarily aggravated circumstances include smuggling, illegal foreign exchange maneuvering, speculating and profiteering for alarmingly high profits, criminal drug trafficking, illegal transportation of precious cultural articles, abduction and selling of human beings, hooliganism, forced prostitution and the illicit manufacturing, trafficking, transporting, or theft and robbery of guns, ammunition, and explosives. The penalties for these crimes enhance the deterrent force of the law as well as the social effect of law enforcement.

The Decisions and Supplementary Regulations have, by way of revision and amendment, provided for the application of maximum statutory punishment and have extended the application of penalties. The weakness of the original Criminal Code, as being too lenient in sentencing and therefore extremely inadequate for prevention and punishment of crime groups and ordinary joint crimes, has been remedied by the increased variety of penalties, prolonged terms of imprisonment, and the mandatory maximum statutory penalties for leaders of crime groups and principals of ordinary joint crimes.

However, the variety of penalties and longer terms of imprisonment is applicable only to extraordinary serious crimes as well as to ringleaders and principals of crimes. That kind of application reflects one of the basic ideas of the Chinese Criminal Law—imposing heavier sentences for ringleaders and principals than for minor criminals. Although life imprisonment cannot be imposed on drug-making and drug-trafficking criminals under the Criminal Law, under the current Anti-Drug Decision, life imprisonment or the death penalty is possible only for ringleaders smuggling, transporting, or making drugs in groups or for criminal participants in organized international drug-trafficking.

The sentencing guideline for crime group ringleaders and principals of aggravated joint crime has been revised, because the amount of value involved in economic crimes is the main basis for sentencing. The current statute, as a result of revisions and supplements under the Decisions and Supplementary Regulations, provides that the ringleaders and principals under aggravated circumstances be punished in terms of the sum total of the amounts involved. It is further provided that if the respective value-amounts involved in joint economic crime computable to the individual participants of the crime are less than the minimum for establishing a criminal case, but if the sum total exceeds the minimum, the principals shall nevertheless be punished accordingly. This new provision will make the punishments severer than they were within the statutory scale of sentencing.

Both the Decisions and Supplementary Regulations, in order to timely reflect the necessity of China's judicial practice and provide necessary legal bases include some new crimes, such as the misappropriation of public funds, imparting criminal modus operandi, and the smuggling, making, selling, or disseminating of pornography. These crimes are often committed by crime groups and in joint crimes.

The legislative intention of heavier punishment for joint crimes committed through collusion and collaboration with government and public office functionaries has been provided under the Decisions and Supplementary Regulations. The People's Supreme Court and Supreme Procuratorate have also given a number of judicial interpretations. Their reply note, "Law Application in Cases of Criminal Tax Evasion Involving Tax Officers," provides that aggravated tax evasion by taxpayers in collaboration with tax officers shall be considered a joint offense of tax evasion; it is punishable by a maximum penalty within the statutory scale of penalties. The provision of the punishment is an addition to the original Criminal Law.

The Criminal Law, the revisions and supplements of the Decisions and Supplementary Regulations and the judicial interpretations of the People's Supreme Court and Supreme Procuratorate have been improving criminal legislation regarding the treatment and punishment for group crimes and ordinary joint crimes. The legislation reflects China's actuality and reality. Group crimes and ordinary joint crimes are included in the statutory grounds for maximum penalties within the legal scale of sentencing. The increase in statutory punishments, new crimes being identified, and the extended application of some punishments to certain crimes have now been included in current criminal enactments which are more systematic and efficient for China's fight against crime groups and ordinary joint crimes.

The Characteristics of Group Crimes

Crime groups in a strict criminal and legal sense are still rare in China. Cases involving crime groups from 1988 to 1990 represent only 1.56 percent of all criminal cases, according to statistics supplied by Shanghai procuratorates. Loosely organized gang crimes, however, are evidently on the increase; 414 individuals, representing 17.9% of those accused for all kinds of crimes from January to April, 1991, were reported in statistics on prosecuted gang crimes in Shanghai; that percentage is 6.29% higher than that of the same period in 1990. Gang crimes have been destructive and corrosive to China's social peace as well as to its social and economical order. Current gang crimes, differing from the gang crimes of hooliganism in the early 1980, have some distinctive features.

In the early 1980s, gang members usually were loosely organized neighbors, co-workers, or friends. In recent years, however, gang crimes are better organized and are mostly well planned before they occur. Many major violent crimes are committed by crime gangs. If not suppressed quickly, these crime gangs will become crime groups.

Recently some long-extinct crimes have reappeared such as drug-trafficking, illicit weaponry deals, for-profit abduction of women and children, gambling, larceny of precious cultural relics, counterfeiting, and prostitution. Because these kinds of crimes require a number of people, it is only natural that gang criminals will be involved in a large percentage of them.

From January to August 1990, according to statistics of the Guandong Provincial People's Procuratorate, there were arrested in Shenzhen, Fushan and Chungshang ninety-six people in twenty-two underworld or quasi-underworld criminal cases. These gangsters were either from the Hong Kong underworld directly or absorbed, trained, and directed on the mainland by the Hong Kong-Macao underworld. Their main crimes include robbery, extortion, and hooliganism against some of Hong Kong-Macao investors on the mainland, private and commercial industries and against construction workers from other parts of the mainland. Individual cases involving quasi-underworld criminal organizations have been reported in Shanghai.

Larcenies represent eighty percent of all criminal offenses in China these days, of which many have been serial larcenies committed by gangs. Of the ninety-one major larceny cases uncovered in Shanghai in 1990; thirty-four were committed by gangs involving 509 serial larcenies. Forty-six percent of the cases involved more than ten offenses. Thirteen larceny gangsters, including Hu Zhijung, all of them peasants from provinces were arrested in 1990. They stole, time after time, from more than ten warehouses in Shanghai; the industrial raw materials they stole were valued at 170,000 yuan. The thefts had been well planned by the gangsters, and trucks and passengers cars were hired to carry the stolen property to illicit buyers.

In criminal activities juveniles comprise the membership of gangs. Some of them, influenced by their "friends," will suddenly commit a crime, acting with cruelty and without caring for the consequences of their crime. They cause great danger to the peace of society. The juvenile criminal gangs have been a social problem deserving grave public concern.

The ringleader of a crime gang is most probably an extremely unscrupulous law-breaker with a previous criminal record. Some of them are ex-convicts; some are subjected to education-through-labor or to administrative sanction for breaking social peace and order; some are still anti-socially inclined; some are vicious criminals. All of them are extremely dangerous to society.

Along local railways and highways many gang robberies have occurred, and the means of transportation have been destroyed. Criminals steal materials carried by railways; some criminal gangs or groups publicly robbed passengers of their property, insulted or even raped women passengers; some armed with weapons even stabbed and injured railway policepersons and passengers. In some areas criminal gangs specialized in robbing freight cars. These criminal gangs, though somewhat repressed as a result of decisive law-enforcement actions taken by the judiciary and local strike forces under comprehensive treatment programs, do occur from time to time.

Crimes committed by two or more legal representatives or members of company businesses or by people posing as them have been new joint crimes. Some members of a business usually offer or take bribes, smuggle or peddle contrabands, speculate, or profiteer.

Procuratorial Practice

As supervisory judicial agencies, the procuratorates in China authorize arrests, examine and initiate prosecutions, supervise the legality of activities of investigative agencies, and supervise the legality of court activities by supporting public prosecution before the courts. The procuratorates also have the power to investigate criminal cases involving office-related offenses of state functionaries and to supervise the legality of the activities of the reform-through-labor agencies and the rehabilitation-through-labor agencies. Since their reestablishment in 1978, China's procuratorates have made great achievements in making sure that laws and decrees are uniformly and correctly implemented, crimes punished, and people protected. In intensively fighting serious criminal and economic offenses, the procuratorates have exercised their full legal powers, actively cooperating with investigating agencies and courts, quickly treating and punishing a large number of serious criminal and economic offenders, and thereby defending the successful development of socialist modernizations. In the 1980s Shanghai procuratorates have paid great attention to the criminal policy of "combining punishment with leniency" in the exercise of their supervisory powers. They attack crime groups and gangs with a policy of education, correction, and dissolution while striking a balance between severity and leniency.

With regard to criminal cases involving major groups and gangs under investigation, the procuratorates shall, according to Article 45 of the Criminal Procedure Law, quickly exercise their supervisory function by referring to files, participating in consultation, learning the progress of the investigation, and reviewing and checking facts. If available evidence is insufficient, the procuratorates shall immediately ask the investigating agencies to make additional investigations within the statutory time limit.

Procuratorates must strictly adhere to law in exercising their powers of prosecution review. While handling cases involving joint crimes, especially group crimes, the procuratorates persistently implement the principle of hearing any such case in toto as prescribed by the People's Supreme Court and the People's Supreme Procuratorate. When the crime facts in a whole case are clear, that case must be prosecuted as a whole, so that an incorrect conviction or an improper sentence can be avoided and so that some accomplices or offenses in the same case may not be neglected.

Persistently focusing their attack on leaders, principals, instigators, and recidivists of crime groups or gangs, the procuratorates must separate from them those who have surrendered or have been coerced or induced and first-timers and petty offenders. For some criminals, the procuratorates will suggest that the courts give them lesser or mitigated penalties. For other criminals, the procuratorates may drop their prosecution or excuse them from prosecution. China's idea is to educate and help the majority of juvenile petty offenders by differentiating them from the leaders in group or gang crimes.

In the prosecution review process, the unswerving course of education, persuasion, and help is applied to juveniles of crime gang and groups. Social forces must be mobilized to educate and supervise those juveniles who are not subject to criminal liabilities. In the meantime, a special trial system and an ad hoc prosecution system have been gradually formed and improved, mostly for the benefit of accused juveniles of crime groups or gangs. The systems facilitate the prevention of crimes and the reform of the offenders by focusing on the correction of the criminal behavior of underaged offenders and on the integration of education and punishment.

In handling cases involving crime groups and gang crimes, the judicial principle of divisions of labor with responsibility, mutual coordination, and checks and balances must be adhered to among the people's courts, the procuratorates, and the public security agencies. Under the current law, when the people's procuratorates discover that some joint offenders, who should be subject to arrest or prosecution, are neglected by public security agencies, they will suggest that the public security agencies apply for orders to arrest or prosecute them. In 1990, Shanghai procuratorates, in examining and approving arrests and prosecutions, suggested to the public security agencies that they refer 157 neglected offenders to the procuratorates.

The application or law varies with various group or gang crimes. In examining those cases, the procuratorates must act in strict accordance with law and must classify gang crimes as either ordinary joint crimes or group crimes. According to the role played by an individual offender in a crime group or gang, that individual is separately charged with a appropriate crime and punished accordingly after public prosecution. In the exercise of judicial supervisory power, the procuratorates handle cases in strict accordance with the law and consider that the sentence of a people's court strikes a good overall balance for the individual offenses in the case and for the conviction and sentencing. The procuratorates can lodge their protest against a court decision, because of an inaccurate characterization of a crime or inadequate sentencing.

The procuratorial departments in detention centers are duty-bound to educate detainee-offenders in that they realize their guilt and willingly serve their sentences. Great care must be taken to differentiate crime leaders from accessories and accomplices and adults from juveniles offenders to achieve "leniency for those who have confessed and severity for those who refuse criminal justice." Juvenile or young offenders are encouraged to "turn back to the right track from the wrong track where they have deviated and lost." Through education—legal and literacy—counseling help, and correction, the procurators have created conditions for the later punishment, education, and correction of juveniles.

To those who have been granted leniency, the procuratorates must pay them follow-up home visits. Shanghai procuratorates pay great attention to such follow-up visits to those who were in joint crimes and were granted leniency, including those excused from prosecution, under probation or surveillance, or on parole. The procuratorates' work is closely coordinated with educational and help groups at residential areas or units. Helping the offenders report their ideology periodically to public security agencies and helping them take care of their life and work and to solve their special difficulties and problems with the cooperation of relevant departments play a positive role in reforming all criminals and preventing crimes.

Shanghai's Transient Crime and Its Countermeasures

by Yuan Yougen

Collective crime or organized crime is one of the relatively obvious phenomena now in the international community. Collective crime usually means well planned, well organized criminal activities planned by a leader and key members in the organization. It has its own rules of behavior and ideology. In comparison with other general crime, it is random, cruel, tricky and harmful. Many collective crime groups and their criminal activities, having crossed borders, have become transactional criminal groups. It is the common task for all police departments in countries and in regions to combat organized crime.

In the past decade, with the implementation of the open door policy in China and with the increase of foreign trading and of international contacts, organized crimes from abroad have taken the opportunity to infiltrate onto China's mainland. The mafia in Hong Kong, Macao, and Taiwan is very active in trading, tourism, real estate, and investing. Generally they commit crimes and infiltrate in many ways.

Shanghai is the largest city of China open to communication with the outside world. It is the most important target for mafia forces abroad to infiltrate, the number of transient or trans-border criminal cases has increased steadily in Shanghai recently, and the number of those group members caught by public security departments has also increased.

Transient crime is committed by criminals from abroad and within China. It is a term accepted through common practice by Chinese police towards criminal infiltration. Transient crime includes two essential elements: the involvement of foreigners or persons from abroad and a criminal offense within Chinese borders. In transient criminal cases, many people are manipulated and controlled by foreign criminal groups with the characteristics of organized crime. Although such cases are not numerous among current criminal cases, transient crime in Shanghai is hard to stop because of its changing and adaptive activities. Because it poses serious dangers to Chinese society, it has already aroused the attention of the Chinese police.

Transactional Crime in Shanghai

During the past several years, basically five kinds of transactional cases have been identified and prosecuted in Shanghai.

The first kind of transient crime is international trafficking of narcotics. Recently, international trafficking groups have tried to open a "passage in China." More and more narcotics trafficking from the "Golden Triangle" went through China to Hong Kong, Macao, Europe, America, and Japan. Some groups worked indirectly in international drug markets; others directly trafficked within China's borders. In almost all prosecuted cases, heroin, opium, and marijuana were to be marketed outside of China. The trend of being more well organized and professional has become increasingly obvious. The criminals have collaborated with one another at home and abroad, from region to region, operating for a long time in conspiracy. They form a professional narcotics trafficking system of dealing, transporting, and marketing. They have secret liaison points to transfer and store narcotics. They use modernized means of communication and are increasingly cunning and secretive. In 1988, the "Golden Carp Case" was found to involve the mafia in Hong Kong. They gave 4.5 kilograms of heroin to runners. The heroin was imbedded in live carp swimming in tanks. The runners transported the fish and drugs from Hong Kong to Guangzhou to Shanghai, intending to make a shipment from Shanghai to San Francisco via international airlines. With the cooperation of American and Hong Kong anti-narcotics agencies, Shanghai agencies cracked the case. Recently, Shanghai agencies cracked another case of marijuana trafficking. A young man from a European country was followed when he was traveling on the ship, *Jian Zhen*, to Osaka, Japan. He was carrying 7.2 kilograms of marijuana paste and was being manipulated by a transactional criminal group.

The Chinese government always pays great attention to narcotics prohibition. Before liberation, foreign invaders once used opium as the tool to plunder the wealth of China and to poison the health of the Chinese people. After the new China was founded, the Chinese government promulgated a decree banning opium smoking and the opium trade, penalizing a number of criminals for narcotics manufacturing, trafficking, and transporting, and outlawing all opium houses. The People's Republic of China was determined to help all drug addicts to give up smoking and therefore terminate one hundred years of opium poisoning. Thirty years ago, the

Chinese government proclaimed that China had eliminated drug-taking. China enjoyed an international reputation as "A Country without Narcotics." However, international drug trafficking groups have recently returned to China with their drugs and criminal activities. Not long ago, China established the National Drug Prohibition Committee. The Standing Committee of the National People's Congress also enacted a Drug Prohibition Resolution which made known the government's determination to eliminate narcotics and to investigate narcotics trafficking wherever it occurs. Now the whole society, including the masses, had been widely mobilized to energetically enforce drug prohibition. The trafficking, producing, and taking of drugs are banned, and prohibition, prevention, and punishment are undertaken simultaneously. At the same time, China is further strengthening international cooperation with the other countries to end all narcotics crimes as they occur.

The second kind of transient crime is swindling not only in trade and business but also in banking and financing, and recently in international maritime affairs. Like swindling cases in other countries, these cases are usually manipulated by international criminal groups. Most of the swindles accomplished in the name of business and trade were committed by using imported and exported goods as baits and through domestic and foreign collaboration. A gang of criminals in Hong Kong, using a false identification of "general manager" of an import and export corporation, collaborated with inland partners and cheated a business in Shanghai. They give false information that large quantities of goods would be sent from Osaka, Japan. By using false commercial certificates and papers, such as a forged supply contract of a certain corporation in Japan and a forged transportation list, they defrauded one business of 9,420,000 yuan. They transferred the money out of the country with the help of partners in Shenzhen and Zhuhai and then absconded to Singapore.

Other transient swindle cases occurred in the use of travellers' checks and credit cards issued by banks of different countries. A criminal group in Hong Kong used various travellers' checks and credit cards, had them taken several times to Shanghai by runners, and drew cash from various exchanges, amounting to more than 70,000 yuan in foreign exchange certificates.

Recently, a swindle case in international maritime business became a new kind of crime arising in China. A ship, *Wei Tai,* loaded at Thailand with goods valued at more than $3,000,000, was originally destined for Singapore. During its voyage, the ship, according to instructions from the swindle group, altered course and sailed to the outer region of Wusong in Shanghai. It was anchored, repainted, and the vessel's name and log book were changed to evade examination. There is a special criminal group in international maritime business in Hong Kong and Taiwan which purchased second-hand vessels at low prices, opened a shipping company in Thailand, recruited sailors, and transported goods. After the *Wei Tai* left Thailand, the criminals who were working at the shipping company, decamped. To them, swindling is a constant occupation; therefore their transient organization is a professional criminal group.

The third kind of transient crime is smuggling. Recently, the foreign criminals have resumed their smuggling activities in the Shanghai area, and their activities have increasingly intensified. The smuggled goods include gold, electronic products, cultural relics, and cigarettes. Foreign smuggling gangs have already spread their activities from special economic zones of Guandong and Fujian to the port of Shanghai. In 1990 foreign criminals rented ocean-going vessels to transport a large quantity of cigarettes to Hua Niao Island in the East China Sea. They then distributed the goods to fishing boats sailing into the Huangpu River in Shanghai. They were finally seized by the Shanghai Police Department.

China is a country with an ancient civilization. The cultural relics from several thousand years of history have aroused the great interest of criminal gangs in China and abroad. By every possible means, they have tried to smuggle cultural relics out of the country to seek exorbitant profits by selling them at high prices in foreign countries. As a result, they dig at the sites of ancient tombs, rob warehouses, and steal from museums. To protect its historical legacy, China must take resolute measures which include international cooperation to severely punish the criminal gangs that smuggle cultural relics.

The fourth kind of transient crime is trafficking counterfeit money into China. The mafia in Taiwan, Hong Kong, and Macao has secretly transported counterfeit bank notes manufactured outside of China and has sold them in large quantities in Shanghai. Criminal cases involving counterfeit U.S. dollars, Hong Kong dollars, Chinese yuan notes, and foreign exchange certificates have been uncovered many times in Shanghai. Harid, a Pakistanian national, and others were ordered by the mafia in Hong Kong to bring counterfeit U.S. dollars into China. They trafficked three times, carrying more than $30,000. The police seized 180,000 yuan in counterfeit foreign exchange certificates which had also been secretly transported into China. Confiscating counterfeit notes is an international problem and is also a common problem for police departments in all countries in the world.

The fifth kind of transient crime is the abduction of women illegally across national borders. The mafia in Hong Kong and Macao use some women's desire to go abroad and abduct them under the pretense of helping them exit or finding jobs for them. Some bought Hong Kong identification cards and returning permit cards, forged the seals, and changed the photographs to allow the women to pretend that they were tourists from Hong Kong. Forging passports, seals and certificates not only creates conditions for illegal exit, but it also provides criminal groups with conveniences. They make the entry into and the exit from China easy with forged passports to evade investigation by police. Consequently, the police from various places must pay close attention to the use of forgeries and fake passports.

Characteristics of Transient Crimes

Transient or transnational crimes in Shanghai are different than those in the Guangzhou District near Hong Kong, Macao, and on the Fujian coastal region near Taiwan. The infiltration by outer-border criminal groups into Shanghai has been for economic gain. Mostly these non-violent cases involve drug trafficking, smuggling, swindling, and trafficking in counterfeit notes.

Most of the criminals are from Hong Kong, Macao, and Taiwan. Among criminals arrested, more than ninety percent are from these regions; most of them have mafia backgrounds. These regions are close to the mainland, convenient to transportation, and easy to leave and enter again. Recently, the direct trade of Shanghai with Hong Kong and Macao has developed rapidly and provides convenient conditions for transient and transnational crimes. Criminals commit economic crimes under the pretense of doing business and trade.

Most of the criminal offenses are committed by criminals in China in collaboration with others abroad. In order to realize their criminal goals smoothly, the criminal groups from abroad induced local criminals in Shanghai with economic bribes, through threats, and with offers of false passports. They make use of their familiarity with the local situation, and these collaborations are usually easily established.

Outer-border criminal groups consider Shanghai as a relay station, from which communications radiate to other cities and areas of the country. They make good use of Shanghai because of its convenient transportation, prosperous economy, its developed commerce, and its dense population. For transient crimes, Shanghai is a transfer station to Southeastern coastal regions, to provinces in the hinterland, and to different parts of the world by air and sea transportation.

Countermeasures

The current transient or transnational criminal activities in Shanghai are becoming more and more complicated, and the characteristics of organized crimes are becoming more and more obvious. These crimes bring great menace to the economic construction and the social security in Shanghai.

China will strengthen its research on international criminal trends and take resolute measures promptly. The world today is an open one. The international criminal phenomena existing in international society change in accordance with world politics and economic situations. Such changes will exert influences upon every open country. Transnational crime is an unavoidable social phenomenon. Therefore, China must intensify its research on the trends and tendencies of organized crimes, because they must be stopped and prevented from reoccurring and expanding. China must learn from the experience of police in other countries in their dealing with organized crimes and must formulate appropriate policies towards different crimes.

China must also intensify its fight against the infiltration of outer-border mafia influences and strike at their criminal activities severely. Early in the 1980s when criminal activities of the mafia were discovered, the police attacked the mafia influences, cracked down on many cases, and punished a number of criminals. However, the mafia was not exterminated. It has been predicted that as long as the outer-border mafia are still active; their criminal infiltration will be unavoidable. China's struggle against the mafia influences will be a long-term fight.

As for Shanghai, although no organizational infiltration of the mafia abroad has been uncovered, many criminals in transient criminal activities were members of the mafia abroad or had mafia backgrounds and were dispatched to commit crimes in Shanghai. China must be vigilant concerning the development of these crimes. China's basic countermeasures for dealing with the infiltration of outer-border mafia influences include never allowing the mafia from abroad to enter China's borders to develop an organization, crack down firmly as soon as they are discovered, never allow cities in the coastal areas or countryside to be harbors for the mafia abroad, and finally, strike resolutely to bring criminals to justice.

Combatting transient crime will be an extended job for Chinese police, and China should pay attention to striking against criminal activities wherever they occur. China must learn more about the nature of transient or transnational crimes through research and investigation. Are these groups organized into factions? What is the range of their influence? What rules of behavior do these groups have? Answers and information should be accumulated professionally and be kept currently.

China should strengthen the reconnaissance of special cases, define them immediately, and crack down on them quickly. Transient and transnational criminals are well organized and are devious in their offenses and anti-reconnaissance. In cases of drug trafficking, smuggling, swindling, and counterfeit note trafficking, inner and outer-border criminals collaborate with each other. Various detection techniques must be used by China in the active reconnaissance of special cases. After having gathered the criminal facts and authenticating evidence, an appropriate time to crack the case and try to arrest the whole gang at once must be determined. How to seize the key members of the collective crime and the leaders who plot behind the scenes must also be determined.

China must strengthen international cooperation in attacking transient and transnational crimes. In China, transient crime specifies certain crime with foreign elements. Internationally, it is usually seen as transnational crime from one country to many countries. From the cases uncovered in Shanghai, organized crime also often appears in foreign countries and regions. There will not be a decisive effect in attacking transnational crimes if China depends only on the forces of one country or one region. It is necessary to strengthen international cooperation, and China must keep in close contact with the police in Hong Kong and Macao, assemble criminal information, uncover transnational criminal cases cooperatively, help seize criminals who have escaped onto the mainland, and prevent them from fleeing and hiding. Governing laws may vary from country to country, from region to region, but with joint efforts of police forces in all countries, China will be able to achieve success.

Gang Crimes in Shenzhen

by Lai Bojin

A gang offense, a particular form of joint offense, is a new type of group offense, but is not entirely identical to joint offense of a group offense. A gang offense has some characteristics or "brotherhood" and of a feudal secret society and is mainly taken as the offender's ideological prop. The gangs are variable and unstable. The gang will not be deemed criminal unless it has taken or is ready to commit criminal acts as stated in the criminal law. Usually the gang offense refers to the joint intentional offense committed by two or more persons. If any person capable of bearing criminal liability participates in a group offense, he or she is considered to have committed a joint offense and to have been a member of a criminal gang. A close investigation of his or her criminal responsibility is made according to the provisions of law.

In addition to theft gangs, robbery gangs have been rampantly committing crimes in various ways. Consequences to society are severe.

In Shenzhen, a city with a million people, the cases committed by robbery gangs from 1989 to 1990 make up 58.7 percent of all robbery cases, and the offenders in robbery gangs make up 76.8 percent of all robbery offenders. These criminal activities not only directly threaten the security of properties but also seriously affect social stability. An analysis of the characteristics and causes of robbery gangs and a study of precautions against them are very important to ensure social stability and promote economic construction.

Characteristics of Robbery Gang Offenses.

China has pursued a policy of opening to the outside world and invigorating its domestic economy. As a result, there has been a great flow of personnel, funds, and materials on the mainland to promote economic prosperity. However, some citizens, motivated by ideas of wealth and pleasure-seeking, defy the Chinese laws and assemble in gangs to commit physical assaults and robberies.

In Shenzhen, the members of the criminal gangs who participate in robbery activities have some common characteristics. A large proportion of people are temporary non-Shenzhen residents; they comprise two-thirds of the city's population. Among these temporary residents and casual workers are some employed persons who do not work steadily and some unemployed persons who have nothing to do. Seeking money and pleasure, they often idle in the streets and await an opportunity to commit offenses. According to city statistics, offenders who are temporary residents and temporary workers account for 71.1 percent of the robbery gang criminals in the city from 1989 to 1990.

A large proportion of juvenile offenders are involved in robbery gangs, and they are getting younger and younger. The offenders under the age of twenty-five, including school students, constitute 93.6 percent of all robbery gang offenders, and the juvenile offenders aged ten to seventeen comprise 25.7 percent of all robbery gang offenders, of whom the youngest is ten years of age.

Some gangs have elements of the underworld in them. Underworld organizations outside the territory of the People's Republic of China take advantage of trade and tourism to infiltrate their personnel into cities and secretly expand their organizations under the protection of legal scrutiny. Therefore, in robbery gangs some offenders, recruited by outside underworld organizations, are directly linked to those underworld organizations.

According to the provisions of Chinese law, articles of property are the objects robbers take. Robbery gangs always reveal their characteristics and patterns when robbing articles of property.

As a result of the extension of China's open-door policy, the rapid increase of the mobile population, and a lack of management experience, some occasional robberies occurred. The offenders' main object was to rob articles of private property, but later robbery gangs wanted a wide variety of property. Losing interest in small robberies, gangs began robbing factories and banks. The robbery gang of six offenders, with Zeng XX its leader, covered their faces with masks and used knives to rob a market of more than 30,000 yuan.

A few years ago, one robbery gang in Shenzhen generally chose to attack residents' houses where articles of property were easily robbed. The increase of both the robbery gangs and the cases against them diverted the gangs from robberies of single houses to collectively using operational vehicles. From 1983 to 1987 thirty-four robberies of taxis occurred in

Shenzhen; in 1988, nineteen robberies of operational motor vehicles occurred; and in 1989, fifty-three vehicular robberies occurred. On October 22-25, 1989, the robbery gang with Chen XX as its principal robbed operational motor vehicles for five successive times.

Usually criminal elements aim at robbing articles of property, but under certain circumstances they even dare to kidnap by force criminal offenders and suspects living at home under the surveillance of judicial agencies. A robbery gang of ten people first resorted to violence and injured Chinese surveillance personnel and then seized some offenders under Chinese prison management by damaging a lock and forcing a door open. The gang had received bribes of 80,000 yuan from underworld personnel outside the territory of the People's Republic of China.

In the past, robbery gangs committed crimes at unnoticed places, but now they brazenly commit robberies openly plundering everything valuable in the daylight. The past cases of robbery occurred at night, and in out-of-the way sections of roads, villages and lanes, or to a single pedestrian. There are now various kinds of robberies. Some gangs conduct criminal activities in broad daylight; some openly rush into shops, hotels, restaurants, and citizens' homes to collect so called "protection fees" for guarding locations. If these fees are not given to the gangs immediately, they will conduct robberies.

In the past criminal elements focused on local citizens in robberies, but they attack overseas travelers and businessmen who often enter China with gold and jadeite articles. These criminal elements are idle in the streets and lanes all day long, and when a gap between their consumption and income occurs, the idea of robbing overseas travellers occurs to them. The XX robbery gang gathered eight criminals together to rob an overseas businessman of valuable articles worth more than 400,000 yuan.

Robbery gangs take "brotherhood" as their ideological prop to muster those persons who ignore their proper occupation in society. These gangs are loosely organized and unstable. As soon as an organization is established, it begins to disband.

Some robbery gangs are temporary organizations in which the membership is not fixed. Before committing a crime, they usually have no plan and when committing a crime, the criminal members are excitable and prone to creating confusion. To join a gang is quite simple. An offering of a cigarette to a youth or a casual meeting may result in membership. After committing a crime everyone who participates is a gang member. One evening, the XX robbery gang gathered in a park and found young couples making love. XXX who was only fourteen years old suggested that "we have nothing to do; let's rob someone of money." Several classmates agreed with XXX's suggestion, and they returned to the park to commit robberies. After distributing the money, the gang casually disbanded.

Robbery gangs can also be revengeful types because of their personal grievances. Casual friends are mustered together to avenge themselves against someone else, according to a plan. A robbery gang with the offender Li X as its principal attacked their victim, Wu X. Li X suffered losses in a business with Wu X, and Li wanted revenge. When Li learned that Wu X had valuable jewelry, he mustered townsmen and colleagues to rob Wu X of a jadeite ring valued at ten hundred thousand yuan.

Robbery gangs can be classified as regional types. They are formed by classmates, townsmen, fellow workers, dancing partners, fellow card players, and neighbors. They come from their native places and from the same trades. These geographical conditions and occupational relations provide conditions for their collaboration, and they are people who like each other. To find an opportunity to earn a living, they get together for robbery. A robbery gang of six people, with Qiu XX as its principal, organized Qui's townsmen and classmates to rob others of articles of property on the principal of "sharing joys and sorrows."

Sometimes regional gangs are associated with gangsterdom; some gangs are formed through the permeation and schemes by underworld societies from outside the mainland. The gangsters are generally temporary residents and those who came to the city from other parts of China. Most members are below the age of twenty-five, and gang leaders are called "Big Brother" and "Second Brother." Regional gangs always have premeditated action plans and purposes before each criminal act. They have a strong organization and commit crimes frequently. They are cunning, cruel, and do not consider the consequences of their criminality. These gangsters usually commit several offenses at the same time. While robbing, they also rape and murder people. These gangs are the most harmful and dangerous to the society. In one regional robbery gang, Zhong called himself "Big Brother," Ye was called "Second Brother" and Hu, "Third Brother." The gang often haunted restaurants, dancing halls, parks, and other public recreational places for robbing and stealing. Having committed thirteen offenses since the gang was formed, they went early in July and on August 30, 1989 to parks with weapons to rob young lovers of their watches, gold rings, and necklaces valued at 10,000 yuan.

Some other gangs have school students as their members, who usually have performed poorly academically and feel as if they are faced with a bleak future. Being snubbed and discriminated against in school, they resort to finding "close friends." Enticed by the most backward students, a number of poorly behaved youngsters form gangs and commit offenses.

In the past, criminals committed crimes with weapons, but they have now adopted so-called "advanced" overseas robbing tricks. Some robbers recruit women members into their gangs by paying them. Then they use these women to lure and to rob victims. A four-person gang led by Yuan, a male, premeditated and investigated before they found someone to rob according to their plan. One night three women entered a hotel and lured a hotel guest to their room. They said they would help him to take a bath and would "play together" with him. When the man was paying them, the women's partners broke into the room and hit the victim in the face. The gang of four tied the victim in the bathroom and robbed his cash and a attache case.

Criminals outside China have been known to smuggle foreign-made anaesthetic drugs by way of business activities in China. One gang from outside of China smuggled in a highly effective anaesthetic through business activities. The gang collaborated with girl friends and prostitutes to seduce some pimps, who taking the drugs, were looted of all their possessions.

Some criminal gangs rob victims of their property by using electric clubs. Jiang, Lu and their five associates told a woman that they could exchange her foreign currency for yuan. She was led to a pre-chosen place and hit by an electric club. When she lost conscience, they robbed her of almost 10,000 yuan.

Criminals like to use motorcycles to launch surprise attacks from which they can flee immediately. Gangs of lawbreakers will ride and hunt people in central city areas from nine to ten o'clock in the evening. Riding their motorcycles, they attack non-accompanied women and tourists on sidewalks or around shops, hotels and restaurants. They snatch purses and wallets in surprise attacks. One gang rode motorcycles to follow an overseas passenger riding in a taxi. When they were driving through an out-of-the-way area, one criminal pointed his pistol at the driver and fired two shots that missed the target. The taxi was forced to stop, and the passenger was robbed of nearly 10,000 yuan.

Causes of Offenses by Robbery Gangs

The main causes of crime by robbery gangs include their lack of legal education. Only a few laws and acts concerning robbery gangs have been enacted in China, but some people lack legal sense because of a lack of publicity. They overlook or even defy the existing laws. Influenced by the bourgeois idea of indulging in creature comforts, some criminals crave material wealth. They do not want to create that wealth through their own hard and honest labor. Once their material cravings cannot be met by their economic conditions, they will run risks and rob.

For a time, obscene books and tapes were traded by gangs in markets. Prostitution also occurred. As some young people are contaminated and corrupted, they break the laws by trading in pornography or by participating in prostitution.

In the past few years, schools have overemphasized intellectual education and the need to enter institutes of a higher degree. They have overlooked moral education and the complete development of students. Some morally and academically poor students have given up on themselves once they lagged behind. Some have lost confidence in life and have been led astray, because they find no warmth in their family and are discriminated against socially.

Countermeasures against Gang Robberies.

To prevent and reduce gang robberies, law enforcement must crack down on the law-breakers of robbery gangs severely and quickly according to the law. Only by punishing criminals severely and immediately can China counterattack their criminal rampancy and curb their criminal offenses. Public security bureaus, procurators' offices, and courts should work closely together to stress "immediately" in every procedure from investigation, cracking a case, preliminary hearing, procuratorial prosecution to the hearing and trial at court. While dealing with criminal cases, some publicity should be done to teach people the lessons of the cases.

Ideologically, China should promote socialist civilization. The administration of culture must be strengthened to create social environment. China also must do a better job in ideological work and use socialist moral standards and laws to regulate people's actions. People must learn to resist the corruption of wrong ideas such as money-worship.

Economically, China should firmly follow the socialist principle of distribution according to work. People should work hard to explore effective ways to restrain unfair distribution among social members caused by non-labor income. China should also educate all citizens, the younger generation in particular, to pursue hard work, thrift, self-reliance, and to respect other people's labor and interests. The society should also protect citizens' rights to work and provide the necessary means for living to those who want to work. As a result, people will not commit robberies, because they lack a basic source of income, nor will they be corrupted by illegally obtained wealth.

Finally, comprehensive preventive measures of all kinds should be taken by every local unit. Factories and company businesses should strengthen the management of temporary residents and casual workers. Leaders should bear the responsibility of the security of society, and contacts should be implemented from unit to unit. All of the society should work toward public security. All party and government departments and units should work jointly to prevent criminal activities and maintain public order. Personnel working in judicial and public security departments should improve themselves so that they will enforce laws justly and handle cases honestly. People's judges, procurators, and police officers should create good working images to impel and deter law-breakers everywhere.

Gang Theft Characteristics and Adjudication Countermeasures

by Liu Tongie

Thefts are the most committed criminal offenses in China. Recently the nature of thefts has changed. In thefts, the number of accomplices involved has increased, and the percentage of gang thefts, defined as being committed by more than three persons, has risen higher than all cases of theft crimes. In a 1990 survey, the judgments rendered in theft cases by the Yangpu, the Hongkou and the Xuhui District Courts— all being district courts in Shanghai—and by the Shanghai Intermediate People's Court indicate that of the total number of theft cases and of the total number of theft criminals, 11.15 percent were gang-theft cases and 26.25 percent were gang theft criminals. In theft cases tried by the intermediate court 23.47 percent of them involved gang theft and 44.49 percent were gang theft criminals. Gang offenses like banditry in particular are very rare and not well defined. However, theft is increasing, and its common characteristics need to be studied. Countermeasures to stop gang offenses need to be formulated so that the crime of theft can be checked effectively and its further expansion can be harnessed.

Almost four-fifths of theft gangs are composed of three or four individuals. Their structure and a small membership make detection difficult and help avoid internal conflicts over what is stolen. Furthermore, their structure meets the gang's needs for an average theft crime. It needs one to watch, a second to commit the theft, and a third to recover the thief and what he has stolen. Membership of gangs is comparatively fixed. Theft gangs are usually composed of kinsfolk, countrymen, relatives, and family members. Although gang members know one another, the average gang usually has no leader. Although one principal may have criminal ideas or may have committed more crimes, he is not necessarily a leader, a chosen chief, or a generally acknowledged major criminal.

Most court cases involve thefts of industrial raw materials, the percentages being 43.61 percent of district cases, and 34.78 percent of intermediate court cases. Since the reforms and the policy of opening up China, the developing economy and expansion in production and capital construction have often led to shortages of industrial materials. Moreover, a large difference exists between state-fixed prices and market prices for these materials. Stealing raw materials probably is an easy job that yields exorbitant profits. Because of the large quantity and open-air storage of industrial raw materials, they are easily accessible to thieves. Theft gangs steal like farmers harvest crops. Furthermore, many township businesses and factories belonging to sub-districts, towns and townships become major purchasers of raw materials, and channels to sell stolen goods are becoming thoroughfares. In some places, channels to steal, sell, and buy were established. In return, this illegal trading has given an impetus to offenses of other kinds, and the theft of raw-materials is reflected in the losses of businesses and companies. In district court cases or intermediate court cases, sixty percent of them involve thefts from businesses and companies. The amount of property stolen is often huge. As stipulated by the criminal law of China, the amount of property involved in a theft is weighed when penalties are considered. As shown by statistics, the individual criminals involved with large amounts (usually more than 5,000 yuan) represented 22.18 percent of the criminals in district court cases of gang theft; the percentage in intermediate cases was as high as 90 percent. These percentages are high, because all offenders mobilize themselves to organize their gangs to commit many crimes and their organizing ability must contribute greatly to their successes. Moreover, relying on their powerful forces they can obtain anything they want, no matter how valuable and how large the object might be. The amount of property a gang member gets from a theft is always large, but the amount of property the theft-gang steals is greater. There are theft cases in which the maximum amount of property involved amounted to as much as one million yuan.

The Chinese society has now become open, and people who once remained home travel freely. With a transient moving population there is a flow of money and material. Some in the transient population are gang thieves. In Shanghai, China's largest cosmopolitan city, in district court theft cases, offenders from the transient population comprise 15.95 percent of the total offenders. In intermediate court cases, however, the percentage increases dramatically to 42.98 percent. These two percentages generally equal the percentage of the offenses of peasants. In district court cases, peasant criminals are 16.34 percent of all offenders and in intermediate court cases, 36.36 percent. The transient population in Shanghai is comprised of peasants who have swarmed into Shanghai with no definite purpose; most of them are surplus rural laborers who come to large cities for jobs or for wealth. When they find neither, they form gangs or join gangs to steal and to make a living.

A surplus of laborers is a characteristic of modern society, especially in societies with socialized mass production and a flourishing economy. When business properties are improperly administered and unequal employment opportunities exist for job-hunters, it is not surprising that jobless offenders first appear in the society, and theft gangs emerge from among them. According to statistics, the percentage of jobless offenders is higher in district court cases than in intermediate court cases, being 37.35 percent and 25.62 percent respectively. The data indicate that unemployment and joblessness are connected with criminal offenses, especially with the crime of theft.

The trials of criminal offenders by the people's courts are meant to reflect the policy of combining punishment with education. The aim of adjudication is to prevent and to reduce criminal offenses. Adjudication does not simply mean penalty or sanction. It also means education, redemption and penitentiary help for the offenders as well as joint efforts by the courts for the comprehensive maintenance of good social order. The people's courts at all levels, with an understanding of the characteristics of theft cases, have not only applied law to these cases but also have worked to stop theft crimes. Gradually, some effective adjudicational countermeasures have also been established.

In the process of a criminal hearing, the people's court must determine facts through evidence and determine differentiated treatments. Preconditioned by clear findings and absolute evidence, the court will take into consideration all of the circumstances of a crime, such as the amount of stolen property, the ways of committing the offense, the harm to the victim as well as his attitude toward confession, the repentant behavior and the restitution of stolen property. After its considerations, the court declares the punishment in accordance with the law. In those cases involving extremely large amounts of property, involving vicious means or great losses to the state, the collective, and citizens, heavier punishment must be imposed on the principals and recidivists, according to the law. To criminals whose circumstances are especially grave, the death penalty may be applied. To first offenders, incidental offenders and those who have confessed or have displayed helpful behavior like voluntary surrender or meritorious service, lenient treatment must be given in accordance with the law. Among ordinary cases, a fixed term of imprisonment is given in 77.34 percent of the criminals cases. In 22.66 percent of the cases lesser penalties are given such as suspension of a fixed term of imprisonment and of criminal detention, exemption from criminal punishment, criminal detention, and public surveillance. Article 67 of the Chinese Criminal Code stipulates, "A suspension of sentence may be pronounced for a criminal element who has been sentenced to a criminal detention or to a fixed term of imprisonment for not more than three years, according to the circumstances of his crime and his demonstration of repentance, and where it is considered that applying a suspended sentence will not in fact result in further harm to society." The suspension of sentences should occur often, because convicts can be supervised and reformed in the community by mass efforts. To those who served well while in prison, shortened imprisonment or parole can be applied. As a result, convicts are encouraged to rehabilitate themselves. Such treatment will probably increase the psychological distance between former inmates and gang members, weaken or eliminate gang cohesion, and help to disintegrate criminal gangs. During adjudication, the people's courts combine crackdowns with prevention and take an active part in the campaign for the comprehensive treatment to good social order. The courts have publicized the law by describing cases newly adjudicated. At the conclusion of a court session or after a pronouncement of judgment, the court often offers some education on the legal system.

Observers are given details of the court deliberations and legal analysis. To help the masses achieve a better result from such publicity work, the people's courts will, according to the characteristic of a region, hold hearings or pronounce judgments. Their hearings may be held at the place of residence of a theft gang or the place where a theft occurred, and some analysis of the crime is made to observers. Consequently, many people will be made aware of the harm of criminal gangs and will join to destroy the social base of gang crimes.

Holding public trials and later publicizing the relevant laws are only two forms in the popularization of law. The people's courts publicize the law by publishing papers, articles, photos; they produce films, poster announcements, and wall newspapers. When some gang theft cases are made known to the public, they can exert a subtle influence on people's minds; they can arouse preventive psychology and function greatly to reduce the possibilities of gang formation as well as limiting gang thefts.

The people's courts, having rendered sentences, never abandon ex-convicts, including people who are given a suspension of imprisonment and convicts who serve reform-through-labor terms. Inspections are made frequently, and persuasion and encouragement are given to them. For those who have real difficulties and reasonable demands, the people's courts are ready to offer help of any kind to solve their practical problems. They are reassured, and they know that the society will not abandon them. The work done by the courts with the theft gang members serves to guide them to future social groups and to avoid relapses.

One factor that encourages thefts is that some factories and business lack safety and protective measures. The people's courts recognize this lack of security and will lose no time to deliver judicial proposals to local authorities for better controls to reduce crime rates. Sometimes, the courts send personnel to localities for return visits and investigation and to learn whether they have improved their administration or not. Discussions are held, when necessary, to exchange useful experiences. The practices of the people's courts have helped to prevent offenses.

China's Approach to Drug Offenses

by Shi Huanzhang

Drug offenses are a universal social phenomena, and they constitute a problem of great concern and interest to all governments and peoples in the world. Drug offenses in China change a great deal from time to time and from place to place. From the late 1970s to the early 1980s when China's policy of opening up to the outside world was initially implemented, the country experienced a resurgence of trafficking in the once long-extinct opium, heroin, and other drugs. Increased international and interregional communications and exchanges as well as the introduction of advanced technological and scientific managements have resulted in some collusion and collaboration between small groups within China and overseas drug syndicates.

The Chinese government has often expressed at international conferences its decisions against drug offenses and its intention to intensely fight drug abuse and drug trafficking. Furthermore, the Chinese government is ready to cooperate with the United Nations anti-drug agencies to achieve great efficiency and success in that fight.

Drug Offenses in China

After the outbreak of the Opium War in 1840, Chinese society witnessed great changes which can be categorized into three historic phases. Phase 1 occurred from the Opium War to the founding of the People's Republic of China (1840-1949). During that time China was deluged with drugs under the exploitation of imperialists, feudalists, and bureaucratic capitalists.

In the mid-18th century, the British government, prompted by its colonialist policy, shipped opium into China through the East India Company to exploit the national wealth of China and to harm the physical and mental health of the Chinese people. After the Opium War, the aggressive imperialist powers and the feudal and bureaucratic warlords joined together to maintain their reactionary rule over China. Many high mandarins, landlords, and suburban gentry made fortunes by ill-gotten gains from illicitly growing poppies, producing opium, operating opium dens, and trafficking in opium. Statistics, compiled in October when the PRC was founded, showed that 15,000,000 mu of land was planted in poppies, and there were 20,000,000 drug addicts, 1,030,000 of whom were in Shanghai alone. In Kunming of Yunan Province where the drug problem was most ferocious, 1,600 opium dens and 50,000 addicts existed.

Phase 2 of China's drug history occurred from the founding of the PRC to the convocation of the Third Plenary Session of the Eleventh Party Congress (1949-1978), during which time all drug problems were resolved. China became a world-recognized country, free of drugs.

In October 1949, the newly established PRC government, in order to protect the people's health and reconstruct and expand the national economy, eradicated the hundred-year deluge of drugs through the implementation of a series of decisive anti-drug measures. In February 1950, Premier Chou Enlai issued the first decree against drugs, "On Strict Prohibition of Opium." The decree not only declared to the world the firm position of the PRC government on drug problems but also basically liquidated drugs from society. The government confiscated drug-addiction related paraphernalia and tools, banned drug dens, punished drug offenders, and educated and helped drug addicts.

Phase 3 of China's history in drugs began with the convocation of the Third Plenary Session of the Eleventh Party Congress in 1978. During the opening up of China and its restructuring, drug offenses returned to China, due to the infiltration and penetration of international drug trafficking syndicates and their outlets.

The 1978 Third Party Session of the Eleventh Party Congress ushered in new developments in socialism in China. Since then China has made achievements in the fields of politics, science, culture, and law. However, with their traditional routes of drug trafficking blocked, international drug trafficking syndicates have taken advantage of the traditional Sino-Burmese border trade fairs to smuggle drugs into China. They have tried to establish a "China trail" for drug trafficking. Illicit drug trafficking and addiction have become prominent social problems, because unscrupulous people in China's society are motivated by the allure of quick material wealth.

Characteristics and Causes of Drug Offenses

In their characteristics and causes, drug offenses vary from country to country and from region to region. In comparison to other countries in the world and with old China, drug offenses in China today have a number of particular characteristics.

In the late 1970s and early 1980s, international drug trafficking syndicates planted poppies in large areas of the Golden Triangle to increase over the years the output of opium and heroin. They also did their best to export large amounts of drugs from the Golden Triangle to Hong Kong and Macao and then to other international drug markets. They even tried to traffic within China, but they often found their traditional routes blocked. In the early 1980s the drug China seized was mainly opium; heroin was very rare. The amounts of opium seized were only tens of hundreds of grams; cases involving thousands of grams were few. In the late 1980s, however, China seized, besides opium, large amounts of heroin; between 1989 and 1990, 2,162 kilograms of heroin were seized. Small plots of land planted with poppies have been discovered, but domestic offenders have been unable to process the plants into heroin. The drugs that are available in China in large quantities and of high quality are almost all smuggled into China by international drug-trafficking syndicates.

In the early 1980s, drug problems emerged only in a few provinces and autonomous regions in Yunan, Guangxi, Sichuan, and Guangdong. In the late 1980s, drug problems emerged with different frequency and intensity, especially in Yunan, the southwestern section of Guangxi, the northwest including mainly Shaanxi and Gansu, Inner Mongolia, the northeast centering on Mt. Greater Xingan, and the coastal area of Fujian to the Hong Kong-Macao-Taiwan area, where the situation is very serious. Drugs seized from these areas amount to more than ninety percent of the national seizure of drugs.

The identification of drug offenders indicated that many of them from Burma, Laos, Thailand, and Hong Kong have international origins. In China, 6,361 drug traffickers, of which 1,398 came form foreign countries, were arrested between 1989 and 1990. There is a tendency for drug offenders to act collectively and professionally; domestic drug offenders, except a small number of old-timers from the old society, are mostly new criminals. Many are juveniles and women, including private businessmen, people waiting for employment, peasants, and factory workers; a few are local petty officials.

Induced and instigated by international drug syndicates, some Chinese citizens will not hesitate personally to challenge the law and are only too ready to risk committing drug offenses for large amounts of money. These citizens, however, induce others into drug addiction. Consequently, out of curiosity or even admiration, the weak-minded become regular drug-takers to find stimulation and excitement.

Recently, drug offenders not only act in groups or collectively in a trans-provincial or trans-municipal scale, but they also have sophisticated plans of action involving up-to-date equipment for communications and transportation. Some have acquired weapons. They strive to establish a clever, hidden, and gradual modus operandi to commit drug offenses.

Drug offenses have damaged the international reputation of China and have impaired the mental and physical health of its people in some parts of the country. As they spread, drug offenses cause other crimes such as homicide, robbery, theft, and prostitution as well as social problems like divorce and AIDS.

China is convinced that the existence and growth of its drug problem is certainly not a minor one, though it is not as disastrous as it was in old China. No large drug organization or market exists in China as they do in some Western countries.

The drug problem in China is a manifestation of the world disaster with drugs and international drug trafficking organizations. Another major cause of the growing drug problem in China lies in the fact that small groups of citizens are mentally and physically influenced by drugs. Because China has been a drug-free country, people are unprepared for the phenomenon of drugs, its dangers, and its serious involvement with international drug syndicates. Drug laws and policies have been rather general and vague; in remote border areas, the anti-drug workforce, financing, and equipment are seriously inadequate to suppress the resurgence of the drug problem. Time will, it is hoped, bring efficiency.

Prevention and Treatment of Drug Offenses

With the present resurgence of drug offenses, the government of China has taken a decisive stand in fighting drug trafficking and addiction by creating anti-drug leadership and organization, strengthening the anti-drug workforce, and providing adequate equipment and funding.

China had created from the central government down to localities anti-drug agencies; their function is to lead and organize the fight against drugs. China has also centrally established the National Anti-Drug Commission which directs unified anti-drug planning, calls periodic joint anti-drug meetings, coordinates anti-drug activities with related agencies, trains anti-drug officers, provides funding and equipment required by anti-drug operations, and promotes international anti-drug cooperation. Local anti-drug agencies have been established in provinces and autonomous regions where drug problems are most severe. In 1988, in cooperation with the United Nations Anti-Drug Fund, China invested 250,000 yuan to build a drug anti-addiction center in Reili county in Yunan Province. The county engaged 1,800 people in anti-drug work and achieved good results. The center was called the Reili Model by the United Nations Anti-Drug Fund expert, Professor Sunnet of the University of Chicago Medical School.

To apply laws to severely deal with drug offenders, China has its current Criminal Law, Penal Regulations for the Punishment of Offenders of Public Peace and Order, and other anti-drug statutes and decrees which have separate provisions against civil and criminal offenses. Recently China promulgated a series of drug-related statutes. The Decree on Severe Punishment for Crimes of Serious Disruption of the Economy and the Supplementary Provision for Criminal Smuggling specify harsh penalties, including capital punishment, for smuggling, trafficking and transporting drugs. In 1990, the Seventeenth Session of the National People's Congress Standing Committee adopted an "Anti-Drug Decision" in which other crimes were defined like the illegal growing of drug-source plants and the illicit holding of drugs. For these drug-related violations, not defined as crimes, culprits may be subjected to education-through-labor or other administrative punishments for their disruption of social peace and order. Many local governments have made anti-drug enactments such as The Regulations for the Administrative Punishment of Drug Offenses in Yunnan Province.

Recently in some parts of China, the illicit growing of poppies has reemerged. Although the areas involved are small and the quantities of drugs limited, the very existence of poppy growing is an important inducement to the trafficking, processing, and taking of drugs. It follows, therefore, that China must confiscate and destroy drug-source seeds and plants and severely punish the cultivators and possessors of them. China must prevent with high efficiency any possible resurgence of drug-source plants in the country.

To check the drug inflow from beyond China's borders, finding and seizing drugs have been increased along the Yunnan and Guanshi borders. From the successful crackdown in 1986 by the public security agency of the Yunnan Province in the international drug trafficking case—4.12—to the breakup in March 1990 of the transnational drug trafficking case—89.11—major achievements have been made in checking and suppressing the infiltration of international drug trafficking organizations.

The civil, health, public security and justice agencies in China have recently in cooperation with the public established 180 clinics and rehabilitation centers for drug addicts and have taken de-addiction measures for addicts. In areas stricken by heavy drug use, local governments will post public notices of compulsory de-addiction treatment for addicts and of time limits for registration. Drug users without addiction will be sent to anti-drug workshops and will be persuaded to stop drug use on a voluntary basis under the supervision of the family, the school, or the work unit. The drug addicts may be confined to special de-addiction institutions for medical and psychological treatment; incorrigible addicts will be subjected to education-through-labor and placed in an isolated environment for compulsory de-addiction. Measures to educate, help, and reform drug users have already met with success.

Multifarious anti-drug publicity and education are important pressing tasks of the overall treatment of drug problems. China instills into the public the knowledge of the harm and injury that drugs can do to the human body. Courses under different subjects are taught in formal school education, and two other courses are offered in school curricula—A History of the Opium War and Modern Chinese Anti-Drug History. The mass media encourages drug offenders to turn themselves in for rehabilitation and promotes an active public alert against drug offenses. The anti-drug law enforcement publicity is further enhanced by justice and public security departments; they resolve anti-drug cases by staging public sentencing and providing anti-drug exhibitions. As a result of extensive, in-depth anti-drug publicity, the public has become anti-drug conscious and ready to fight against drug offenses.

To promote international anti-drug cooperation, China has acceded to the Convention on Illicit Trafficking of Narcotics and Psychotheraputical Medicine of the United Nations, has increased the exchange of information and the cooperation among China, Burma, Thailand, and Hong Kong. China's comprehensive national program on the treatment of drug problems is based in part on the United Nations Anti-Drug Fund's recommendations. China also actively coordinates anti-drug enforcement within all of its jurisdictions. In view of the drug bases in the Golden Triangle and the activities of the internationally organized drug operations, China suggests that the United Nations anti-drug agencies study the feasibility of establishing in China an Asian-Pacific drug-testing center and anti-drug laws enforcement training center. These centers would improve anti-drug techniques and accumulate anti-drug experience and skills. At the same time, all the countries and regions located in the Golden Triangle could immediately reach bi- and multilateral anti-drug agreements and join forces to regulate international and inter-regional jurisdiction over drug offenses, extradition, and other related legal problems. Such efforts would escalate national and regional anti-drug activities of the countries and regions involved.

Drugs are not only a continual international problem and a great social concern, but they are also an important subject for comprehensive research of common concern and interest to international lawyers, criminologists, and the criminal justice community. The task of stopping drug offenses is a long term and difficult one, but China is ready to adopt punishment and prevention of drug offenses as fundamental strategies for social stability; they are part of China's systematic social engineering of comprehensive treatment.

Money Laundering in Asia

by Mark Gaylord

For Chinese wishing to relocate eventually in the West or in Southeast Asia, Hong Kong has long been a way station. The British Colony's transient population has been mostly comprised of Cantonese who originate from the region around the city of Guangzhou just north of Hong Kong, and their language and culture dominate city life. Part of the Cantonese heritage includes a tradition in organized crime almost a hundred years old. The Triads, composed of secret societies, originally were part of a patriotic resistance movement of ethnic Chinese who protested political domination by northern Manchu rulers.

When Dr. Sun Yat-Len established the Chinese Republic in 1911 emphasizing nationalism, democracy, and the people's livelihood, the Triads came forward to assist him. Afterward the Triads retrogressed and became little more than criminal bands. In his bid to control China, Sun's successor, Chiang Kai-shek, repeatedly turned to the Triads who by the middle decades of the twentieth century were unlawful tribal groups heavily involved in opium trade. Chiang, like Dr. Sun, were initially Triad members, politically and financially protected by generals, soldiers, spies, businessmen, and hired thugs in the Kuomintang, or better known as the Chinese Nationalist Army. After the successful Communist Revolution in the late 1940s, Triad groups were virtually eliminated in the People's Republic of China. Triad drug dealers were arrested and imprisoned; many were summarily executed, typically by a bullet in the back of the head. Current assessment generally agrees that the Communist Revolution ended China's nightmare of opium addiction. It did not, however, extinguish the Triads. Wherever Chiang's army fled, the Triads went: Hong Kong, Taiwan, China's southern ports connected to the Golden Triangle, and other parts of Southeast Asia.

After World War II, Hong Kong once again was controlled by the British, and Triads extended their influence into the colony, substantially aided by the immigration of fellow members fleeing the mainland. For at least a decade, the British viewed the Triads and other groups as useful in helping to integrate the hugh rush of refugees into Hong Kong. However, the British made a grave mistake by banning opium in Hong Kong. Their policy gave rise to a thriving black market that provided a steady source of income to postwar gangs. Inevitably local Triads increasingly played a central role in the world's narcotics trade. Now Hong Kong-Chinese syndicates smuggle more than half of the heroin reaching the west coast of the United States. Some American law enforcement officials remain convinced that

Chinese syndicates form today's major multinational link to organized crime.

The Golden Triangle

Hong Kong's Triad societies have grown in part because of the city's proximity to the Golden Triangle. The colony's drug syndicates control a vast amount of Southeast Asian heroin from that fabled, borderless region encompassing hill tribes and medieval warlords indigenous of Burma, Laos, and Thailand.

Despite concerted international efforts to halt international drug trafficking and the expenditure of more than ninety-eight million U.S. dollars in aid since 1972, criminal activities in the Golden Triangle persist in providing over fifty percent of the heroin brought into the western coast of the United States and sixty to seventy percent of the heroin docked in New York City. Although drug production in Mexico and Southwest Asia's Golden Crescents—Iran, Afghanistan, Pakistan, and India—remains enormous, many American narcotic dealers continue to prefer the high quality heroin from the Golden Triangle.

Hong Kong refined much of the region's opium during the 1960s; the colony today serves as an entrepot and financial center for the area's narcotics traffic. Serious studies by United States officials in the 1980s revealed that Panama is the outlet for cocaine traffic, as Hong Kong is the outlet for heroin traffic. The Golden Triangle nurtures the opportunity for immense profits which substantially affect Chinese criminal organizations. These profits, laundered in Hong Kong by willing bankers, are secretly shipped abroad and are beginning to be found in San Francisco, Toronto, Vancouver, and New York City.

Hong Kong's Banking Industry

Hong Kong's banking industry acts as a conduit for drug money between that city and the United States. Traffic among large-scale American importers and distributors and Chinese drug traffickers, diversifying their assets by investing in North America, increases daily. No one knows the amount of laundered money emanating from Hong Kong because of the colony's secret banking acts. However, in August 1985, United States Treasury officials fined California's Crocker National Bank $2.5 million for violating the U.S. Bank Secrecy Act; the bank had failed to report during the past five years thousands of cash transactions ultimately totalling almost four billion dollars. Almost all of the money came from six Hong Kong banks. Throughout the proceedings, Crocker's general counsel naturally remained outraged at any suggestion taken by the Treasury Department that dirty money had been laundered through the Crocker National Bank.

Concerned about the large flow of money from Hong Kong the United States President's Commission on Organized Crime as early as 1984 requested the Treasury Department to analyze all available data relative to financial transactions between the United States and Hong Kong. The results computed in United States currency figures were striking; a phenomenal quantity of United States dollars, especially in small amounts, were being sent to and from Hong Kong.

Half of this currency is shipped to the United States, but the balance is transported to other countries such as Switzerland. One-hundred dollar bills exemplify approximately sixty-five percent of the currency repatriated to the United States. However, to informed U.S. enforcers, the movements of small denominations really represent the telltale signs of drug trafficking and money laundering. Their suspicions were confirmed when drug syndicates diverted their earnings in the form of small bills to foreign banks. Overseas banking concerns coverted funds by moving them under assumed names to U.S. banks via wire transfers. Essentially the overseas banks exchanged small bills into larger ones through economic technology with U.S. banks. The consistent increase of U.S. currency repatriated from Hong Kong to the U.S.

between 1982 and 1984 makes this data particularly noteworthy to law enforcement agencies, because it dramatically correlates with the increases in the Southeast Asian-U.S. heroin market during roughly the same period.

Although other logical explanations may account for the annual repatriation of hundreds of millions of U.S. dollars in small denominations from Hong Kong, the President's Commission on Organized Crime concluded that little credible evidence exists to explain this repatriation in any other way. This volume of small denomination bills exceeds the total volume of all currency transactions of any European country. In 1982 the total transfer of United States currency to and from Germany amounted to $12 million; from France, $9 million; from Hong Kong, $100 million. Germany and France could reasonably be expected to have had more tourist traffic and non-business contacts with the United States than did Hong Kong. Moveover, the Treasury Department data revealed a minimal flow of United States currency to Hong Kong in comparison to the flow of United States currency from Hong Kong. Although the Treasury Department cites no evidence to support the conclusion that the surplus of United States currency in Hong Kong results from Southeast Asian drug trafficking, that conclusion remains the most compelling explanation for the inordinate surplus.

Money Laundering

All this money is apparently going to San Francisco. Treasury Department figures show that between 1980 and 1984 the amount of cash flowing to the United States from Hong Kong increased ten times to more than $1.7 billion, of which almost seventy percent had gone directly to the San Francisco area. After a decade of running cash deficits, the Federal Reserve Bank in San Francisco began in 1981 to accumulate huge surpluses which almost tripled by 1985. By the end of 1985, San Francisco's Federal Reserve Bank had posted the second largest surplus of cash, surpassed only by Miami, in the entire federal system.

Hong Kong's favorable geographical position provides a bridge in the time-zone differences between North American and Europe. It developed into a significant international financial center due to its strong connections to China and Southeast Asia and its excellent communications to the rest of the world. By 1990 more than 160 licensed banks were located in Hong Kong of which seventy-five percent were foreign corporations. Foreign banks in Hong Kong represent almost every major country in the world and include seventy-six of the world's one hundred largest banking firms. A substantial proportion of the banking transactions in Hong Kong is thus international in nature.

In addition to standard banks, thirty-five licensed and 232 registered deposit-taking companies were operating in Hong Kong at the end of 1987. Somewhat similar to American savings and loan firms or British building societies, these institutions offer no checking accounts, require minimal assets, permit loans, pay higher rates of interest than banks, and provide wire transfer authority. Deposit-taking companies and banks represent only two types of financial institutions. Hong Kong in 1980 further listed more than 140 offices representing foreign banks and more than 6,000 licensed stock and commodity brokers and investment counsels.

Most attorneys augment Hong Kong's financial industry by specializing in international business and finance. Traffickers find their legal expertise essential in establishing false companies, in purchasing property and ships, and in moving money. Lawyers shroud their activities in anonymity by administering trust accounts and business details.

A very important concomitant of Hong Kong's financial infrastructure has been that of the underground family-operated banking system which exists outside the commercial banking sector yet largely accounts for the means to transfer significant amounts of money to Hong Kong. Almost exclusively controlled by globally connected Chinese families, the system frequently has operations such as gold shops, trading companies, and money exchanges around the world. The system developed from a historical Chinese distrust of banks, political turmoil, and Communist takeovers in many countries where the Chinese resided and were constantly harassed. The Chinese, out of necessity, developed a business style that to Westerners appears extremely secretive. Bitter experiences, however, taught the Chinese that families constitute the only reliable conduit for business.

Record-keeping procedures remain nearly nonexistent for underground banking systems. Coded messages, chits, and simple telephone calls can transfer money from one country to another. The system inherently provides anonymity and security to its customers. Commercial bank facilities augment underground systems when money must be transferred to Southeast Asia from Europe or the United States.

Chinese criminal organizations control most of the heroin trade in Southeast Asian. Their underground banking systems coupled with a web of ethnic-based commercial contacts create a nearly impenetrable maze for law enforcement officials. A Hong Kong police official stated that he once seized from a local gold shop a piece of paper with the picture of an elephant which represented collection receipts totalling three million dollars. Wire taps placed on some of the major gold shops and trading companies by both Thai and Hong Kong police have documented large transfers of suspected drug money.

A Secret Financial Jurisdiction

Because Hong Kong does not maintain a central bank or some kind of currency exchange control, funds entering or leaving Hong Kong cannot be traced. A person can literally and legally carry a suitcase stuffed with money into Hong

Kong. Hong Kong law essentially protects the colony's status as a secret financial jurisdiction.

The jurisdiction minimally seeks to preserve Hong Kong's safe-haven status for billions of dollars not derived from drug trafficking and other criminal activities. However, investors moving money to an offshore jurisdiction run the risk of being in a jurisdiction lacking strict government control in policing potential fraud. Hong Kong nonetheless satisfies requirements of secrecy within its fairly well-regulated banking system, particularly if a customer invests only with one of the colony's major financial institutions. Hong Kong's bank secrecy laws bar oversight by both national and foreign authority. The law declares certain records held by financial institutions to be confidential. Disclosure of data contained in such records may create civil or criminal liability. Statutes further fortify Hong Kong's jurisdictional status by effectively preventing disclosure, copying, inspection, or removal of documents located in Hong Kong, even when a requesting foreign authority complies with court orders. These statutes further prohibit residents of a colony from disclosing certain information or records to nonresidents.

Money Laundering and the Law

Drug traffickers are the major consumers of money laundering services. Like good business people everywhere, they prefer to diversify their assets and invest in legitimate businesses. Consequently, they need to conceal the connection between their moving global funds and the crimes that earned them. Once in an anonymous bank account in a secret jurisdiction, cash can be safely invested for the customer's benefit. To deceive law enforcement officials about a paper trail, money can be easily moved from account to account or bank to bank.

American law enforcement agents continue to be at a severe disadvantage when they try to collect information and evidence of American crimes committed abroad. Legal barriers, including financial secrecy laws, prevent law enforcement agents from examining financial records in Hong Kong's jurisdiction. Although Hong Kong law enforcement officials do occasionally gain access to banking records by proving a reasonable request to the courts, the colony's banking laws do not permit exploratory expeditions into the criminal use of banking accounts. Both American bankers and United States Consulate officials based in Hong Kong observe that the colony cannot guarantee complete secrecy, but by American standards, that secrecy appears extremely rigid.

A banking industry the size of Hong Kong's obviously deals in tremendous sums of money from every conceivable kind of commerce. Local bankers understandably become rather sensitive to accusations of possible drug links to the money in their industry. Although they readily concede that their organizations routinely deposit large sums of United States currency in West Coast banks, they claim the funds largely represent daily foreign exchange transactions with residents of the Philippines, Taiwan, Singapore, Thailand, and other countries in the region. Less agreement exists over the currency flowing through the system generated from the drug trade.

Current Status of Money Laundering

Hong Kong bankers and government officials vehemently reject the notion that their colony symbolizes the world's leading money laundering center. However, in announcing a $2.5 million fine to the Crocker National Bank, the United States Assistant to the Treasury strongly suggested that the bank's holdings resulted from criminal activity. Crocker officials, Hong Kong bankers, and Chinese administrators objected to the allegation.

Hong Kong bankers argued that the large amounts of cash flown to San Francisco simply represented favorable airline schedules that allowed money to be deposited to earn same-day interest.

The United States government claims the money comes from drug trafficking. The Hong Kong government would argue that the money was moved in the early 1980s, because Hong Kong dollars fell precipitously before the signing of the Joint Sino-British Declaration which outlined Hong Kong's future in 1977. An official Hong Kong argument suggests that the movement of United States dollars represents a natural consequence of the colony's increasing stature as the main financial center for all countries in Southeast Asia.

The Hong Kong position makes a strong case for the exceptional quality of the colony's banking system. However, Hong Kong's avenues for money laundering cannot be ignored. Several years ago the government in Hong Kong admitted to some problems with money from drug trafficking. The Narcotics Bureau in 1989 established a financial investigation group to explore these problems, and the Drug Trafficking Recovery Proceed Ordinance was also passed. Hong Kong recognizes the problems and has taken some steps to deal with them, but those steps are too small and come too late. Hong Kong banking regulations must change before any noticeable improvement will be seen in the system. Bankers hesitate to change regulations, fearing that their business would be lost to other secret jurisdictions in Southeast Asia and elsewhere. In the end, money laundering in Asia continues unimpeded by cooperative, international legislation.

Drug Trafficking and Abuse in Hong Kong: A Situation Report

by David Hodson

Hong Kong's history of opiate abuse began in the early part of the twentieth century when opium became the preferred drug of abuse. In the late 1920s heroin abuse was occurring, and by the late 1940s, it was being used more than opium. Since 1930s, heroin, in its various forms, was the colony's most widely abused, illicit drug. A small number of addicts still use opium; however, recent psychotropic substances, such as herbal cannabis, has gained popularity with young drug abusers. The Royal Hong Kong Police remain cognizant of all these drug abuse variations and most aspects of drug trafficking which international cooperation has helped to combat.

An Overview

Hong Kong, located near South China's Golden Triangle opium-producing regions, possesses modern communication and transportation systems. These systems make Hong Kong a natural transit point for shipping Southeast Asian heroin to markets in the West. Because Chinese groups and individuals in heroin-producing regions know their counterparts in other countries, it remains unsurprising how Hong Kong criminal entrepreneurs became heavily involved in the lucrative drug trade. Moreover, more than 140 international banks and finance institutions with advanced facilities are registered in the colony. Undoubtedly they attract business to the area.

The Hong Kong government implemented the 1989 Drug Trafficking Ordinance to enable law enforcement agencies to recover drug traffic proceeds after a trafficker's conviction. The Ordinance also places an obligation on banks and financial institutions to report transactions which they suspect involve drug trafficking. The Ordinance provides that other countries—those that entered into a bilateral agreement and have been designated by Hong Kong as a participating entity—may confiscate in Hong Kong drug traffic proceeds which belong to persons convicted of drug trafficking offenses in another country. Several countries have signed such agreements, and discussions continue with other countries to do the same.

Drug officers recognize that Hong Kong represents a financial center and transportation point for heroin destined for the West. They strive to cooperate with law enforcement authorities in countries that are sources and destinations of drugs and through which drugs are transported. The Territory remains proud of its work record and continues to enhance liaison efforts with enforcement agents in other countries.

Types of Drugs

Heroin is a popular drug available illegally in Hong Kong. Historically, the hard granules of No. 3 heroin, manufactured from morphine, heroin base, or No. 4 heroin, represent its most common form. A fairly simple process to make No. 3 heroin consists of diluting No. 4 heroin with caffeine and adding small quantities of strychnine and quinine. No. 3 heroin accounts for less than ten percent of today's street seizures, and its purity averages two to three percent. More than ninety percent of street seizures involve sixty-five percent pure No. 4 heroin. Hardened drug users inject the drug; new users inhale it.

During the 1970s and early 1980s, cannabis use attracted expatriated Hong Kong residents and Westernized Chinese. The use of herbal and resinous cannabis dramatically increased during the late 1980s, particularly among teenagers and young adults.

Cocaine abuse in Hong Kong also appears to be increasing. Although cases remain rare, evidence shows cocaine abuse becoming widespread within the Territory despite its high cost. One gram of cocaine sells for 1,500 Hong Kong dollars—equivalent to 190 United States dollars—in comparison to 600 Hong Kong dollars for one gram of No. 4 heroin. In the first four months of 1991, police seized 400 grams of cocaine.

For at least two decades, methylamphetamine in both powder and fine crystal form represents another drug sold in small quantities. Legitimately produced in China from organic ephedrine for use as a herbal medicine, methylamphetamine is also mass-produced and shipped by way of Hong Kong to lucrative markets in the Philippines, Japan, and the United States. The d-methylamphetamine hydrochloride composition in the drug called "ice" in the United States is the same chemical structure as was found in Hong Kong.

For several years in the 1980s, psychotropic substances imported from China in powder and tablet form gained popularity among Hong Kong's youth. Chinese authorities imposed strict controls in 1986, and seizures dropped dramatically. Small quantities continue to remain available as do barbiturates, such as Seconal, Benzodiazepines, Valium, Rohypnol, and Halcion. Authorities scrutinize how doctors prescribe these drugs.

Hong Kong's Central Registry collects data from a variety of agencies. Their records reveal that nearly 40,100 people have used drugs at least once in the past five years, and these people are considered active users. Of the total, nine-three percent use heroin, and thirty percent of the users under the age of twenty-one use cannabis.

The International Scene

The Territory unwillingly acts as a conduit for shipments of Golden Triangle heroin to other parts of the world. An overland route also exists from Myanmar to China's provinces of Yunnan and Guanxi and then continues to Guangdong and Hong Kong. Both sea and land routes remain popular. In September 1989, 420 kilograms of No. 4 heroin were seized; they had entered Hong Kong by sea from Thailand. Informed observers predict that Hong Kong's increasing vehicular and pedestrian traffic from China will raise the desirability of using overland routes.

Heroin exported from Hong Kong reaches established markets in North America, Australia, Europe, and, to a lesser extent, other Southeast Asian countries. Air transportation remains the predominate way to export drugs, and air couriers avoid suspicion from countries of destination by taking circuitous routes. Some couriers procure drug cargos by traveling by land to Guangdong; they then carry the drugs to Beijing before flying to drug-consuming countries. Their indirect routes avert suspicion upon arrival in a consumer country and prevent Hong Kong officials from tracking the courier. In sea and air freight leaving Hong Kong, officials have found heroin concealed within legitimate shipments of furniture, in tins of lychee, and in bottles of soy sauce destined for Canada and the United States.

Hong Kong Triad societies and their international affiliates continue to be involved in drug trafficking. The affiliates work with, but are not members of the Triads. By pooling resources, however, these two groups arrange increasingly large and sophisticated imports and exports of heroin. Both the intent of, and the result from, these drug ventures appear to be the accruing of individual profits based upon one's contribution to the venture's success. From all accounts, profits are not channeled through a syndicate or Triad society.

Financial Investigations

Law officers conducting financial investigations are aided by current legislation and seek increased international cooperation. Hong Kong's 1989 Drug Trafficking Ordinance replicates in significant ways the United Kingdom's 1986 Drug Trafficking Offenses Act. Both provide for tracing, restraining, confiscating, and recovering proceeds derived from drug trafficking.

Law officers and customs officials initially prepare background checks on people suspected of drug trafficking. When warranted, law enforcement agents petition the District or High Court for a production order or a search warrant. Petitions may be requested against an institution or individual, and no evidential time limit exists for a confiscation proceeding. Consequently, an officer may furnish historical data about a defendant's drug trafficking which lends prosecutorial weight toward a defendant's current offense and conviction.

The 1986 Ordinance provides that an Attorney General, upon sentencing a drug trafficker, may solicit the High or District Court to execute a confiscation order for remuneration. The courts assume that all property accrued to a defendant during the past six years has been acquired from drug trafficking.

The Ordinance also permits Hong Kong legal groups to assist other countries in their drug trafficking investigations by releasing pertinent information. Requests must be based on reasonable grounds, must be of substantial value to an investigation, and must be in the public interest. For a bona fide application, a production order or search warrant will be issued.

Hong Kong designates which countries may participate in its information exchange program by getting a country to sign a bilateral agreement. Hong Kong's governor, in ruling favorably for a confiscation order against a person from another country holding assets in its Territory, thereby applies Hong Kong law to the case. Again, this Hong Kong law applies to restraining or charging of property, obtaining production orders to determine beneficial ownership, and confiscating such property. Information exchange and mutual assistance support all phases of the investigative effort prior to issuance of a confiscation order.

International Cooperation

Minimal statutory guidelines beyond the 1986 Ordinance exist to indicate how Hong Kong might share drug trafficking information with other countries. The following principles, employed solely in intelligence and investigative work, suggest that requests for information must include what mandates the request and the nature of the investigation; release of information must not compromise a local investigation underway; requesters must not jeopardize an information source; furnished information must not be reproduced or forwarded beyond the addressee, without the originator's consent; and information remains security-graded and is provided on a non-attributable basis.

Search warrants represent another means for law enforcement officials from other countries to enlist assistance from the Hong Kong police. The kind of service provided, however, depends upon whether the crime was committed in Hong Kong or in some other country.

A formal request, such as an Evidence Ordinance, contains statutory requirements. To aid evidential criminal proceedings, Hong Kong's High Court may issue orders to facilitate witness availability and process information-release documents to aid a court case in another country. At times, Hong Kong police testify in another country's courts. The country requesting evidence from Hong Kong must have drug trafficking evidence relative to a specific case prior to seeking Hong Kong government assistance.

Section 25 of the 1986 Ordinance instructs banks and financial institutions to disclose suspected drug trafficking transactions to the police. Although Section 25 remains vague, furnishing information to another country's law enforcement agency, institution, or individual challenges the law.

A literal reading suggests that little information can be furnished to law enforcement groups in other countries. However, an execution order, search warrant, and production order request from another country, based on previously acquired financial evidence, overrides the limitations of Section 25.

Joint Investigations

Concerted efforts between Hong Kong police and those of other countries have become an essential component in combatting drug trafficking. The Royal Hong Kong Police Narcotics Bureau has been and continues to be involved in such efforts.

Generally, joint investigations occur when agencies become aware that they are researching the same syndicate or individual. Mutual intelligence work and information exchanged between agencies help to prepare a successful prosecution in one or the other's jurisdiction. Sometimes an operation to thwart some future criminal activity is begun.

The location of past offenses and each jurisdiction's legal restrictions about extradition are taken into account.

If cooperating agencies orchestrate an operation against a future drug trafficking project, they usually arrange for a controlled delivery which results in seizing both the drugs and the traffickers. Hong Kong police advocate controlled deliveries as an effective ways of capturing violators. They provide full cooperation to enforcement agencies from other countries for controlled deliveries.

Generally Hong Kong officials conduct controlled delivery operations by employing some guidelines. Drugs destined for another country should have an identified recipient. Drug consignments consisting of two or more kilograms will be replaced by a similar substance prior to delivery. If a drug courier agrees to assist police in a controlled delivery operation, a background check must be done before the operation proceeds further. The courier must sign a statement indicating voluntary participation to ensure his return to Hong Kong for trial after the operation has been completed. Defecting couriers normally are granted partial immunity. Early consultation remains vital to the success of a controlled delivery operation.

The current drug trafficking and abuse problems in Hong Kong can be solved, and the Royal Hong Kong Police are ready to offer their knowledge, practical expertise, and assistance to police in other countries.

PART II

GLOBAL PERSPECTIVES

The United Nations Role in Crime Prevention

by Julio Heredia

The United Nations, recognizing the international need to study crime prevention and the treatment of offenders, assumed a leadership position in those areas with Res/E/155. C(VII), 13 August 1948 (ECOSOC).

Two years later, the General Assembly authorized its Secretary-General to transfer the functions of the International Penal and Penitentiary Commission to the United Nations. The new organization agreed that an international congress would continue to convene every five years to discuss global crime prevention. Thirty-five years later, the Seventh United Nations Congress on the Prevention of Crime and the Treatment of Offenders adopted "The Guiding Principles for

Crime Prevention and Criminal Justice" which reiterated that the United Nations should remain the logical center for international cooperation. The responsibility for cooperation was stated again in December 1990 when the General Assembly approved Resolution 45/121.

The objectives of the current United Nations program include assisting member states in reducing criminality and in establishing basic standards and norms for the administration of justice. The assistance includes observations of human rights standards by promoting high levels of fairness, humanity, and professional conduct. The program consequently reflects the purposes of the Charter of the United Nations and, in particular, acknowledges the commitment of all members to take both joint and separate action in following organizational guidelines. By enlisting cooperation, the United Nations endeavors to achieve solutions to international problems of an economic, social, cultural or humanitarian character.

The Branch

The Crime Prevention and Criminal Justice Branch of the Center for Social Development and Humanitarian Affairs at the United Nations Vienna office serves as central repository within the United Nations system. It provides technical expertise in crime prevention and criminal justice, criminal law reform, and major criminological concerns.

Accordingly, the Branch completes research and operational functions entrusted to the Secretariat by the policy-making bodies of the United Nations, such as the General Assembly and the Economic and Social Council. The Branch promotes programs encouraging international cooperation and coordinates transnational, preventive crime agendas. It develops guidelines and standards for the administration of justice and the humane treatment of offenders. It designs strategies to reduce crime and delinquency, thereby limiting their adverse effects on the development process, and it undertakes surveys of crime trends and criminal justice operations. Each of these administrative efforts aids in identifying emerging criminal patterns and helps to shape policy options for improving the management of criminal justice systems.

The Branch further provides guidance for the protection and treatment of juveniles and victims of crime; functions as a clearinghouse for the exchange of information among a worldwide network of criminal justice institutes, researchers, and practitioners; assists member states in implementing existing United Nations policy recommendations; and aims at improving the effectiveness and fairness of criminal justice by providing advice and technical cooperation upon request.

Another responsibility of the Branch includes rendering service to the Committee on Crime Prevention and Control of the Economic and Social Council and organizing the United Nations quinquennial crime prevention congresses. The Eighth Congress was held in late 1990.

Technical cooperation in all aspects of criminal law and management may be obtained from the Branch. Two noteworthy services are also available: advisory missions which provide detailed recommendations at the national level on implementation of United Nations standards and guidelines and other missions which formulate specific projects in respect to diverse aspects of crime prevention and criminal justice.

The Branch furthermore becomes instrumental in the implementation of training programs, study tours, and fellowships to help developing countries in the procurement of equipment.

The functions of the Branch make clear that as the most appropriate clearing center for crime matters, the United Nations shares data with member states and provides a wide range of technical assistance. Unfortunately, resources are woefully lacking to implement these activities. The General Assembly, however, recognizes that the Crime Prevention and

Criminal Justice Branch represents the only professional and specialized entity within the United Nations system with overall responsibility for its crime prevention and criminal justice programs. The Assembly has repeatedly recommended that the Branch should be strengthened in terms of human and financial resources.

Congresses

As expressed in the Guiding Principles, the quinquennial United Nations congresses on crime are designed to promote an exchange of knowledge and experience among specialists from different States and to strengthen developmentally international and regional cooperation in the fight against crime. The latter is done through the adoption of policy-oriented recommendations, guidelines, and minimal standards which the General Assembly, as the supreme United Nations legislative body, endorses.

The overall preparatory and coordinating efforts for these congresses remain the responsibility of the Branch. These activities include interregional meetings of experts, regional preliminary meetings, and other relevant activities.

Institutes

The United Nations, meeting in Rome in 1968, created a global network of institutes for the prevention of crime and the treatment of offenders. Since then, one interregional and four regional institutes have been created. The one interregional institute refers to the United Nations Interregional Crime and Justice Research Institute. The four regional institutes are: The United Nations Asia and Far East Institute for the Prevention of Crime and the Treatment of Offenders; the United Nations Latin American Institute for the Prevention of Crime and the Treatment of Offenders; the Helsinki Institute for Crime and Control, affiliated with the United Nations; and the African Regional Institute, established in 1987, for the Prevention of Crime and the Treatment of Offenders.

In December 1990, the General Assembly during its forty-fifth session reiterated that the United Nations regional and interregional institutes should further develop their research, training, and technical assistance capacities, and widen their collaborative networks through extensive reliance on non-governmental organizations and national research and educational institutions. These efforts would meet the growing requests from developing countries for technical and scientific assistance. Financing, however, would depend entirely upon member states' donations which would contribute to an institute's long-term effectiveness.

The General Assembly's contribution remains crucial in furthering extensive and cost-effective, regional and global cooperation. New efforts have to be made to improve collaboration between United Nations institutes and their respective, intergovernmental and non-governmental organizations. New, reliable ways of funding will also need to be explored.

Committee on Crime Prevention and Control

The Committee on Crime Prevention and Control is the group of experts entrusted with the formulation, guidance, and supervision of the United Nations program in crime prevention and criminal justice. The Economic and Social Council selects twenty-seven experts for this committee. Although the nominations have to be supported by the government of each candidate, the elected experts strive toward impartiality rather than acting solely as government representatives.

The committee has the task of supervising the preparation of the quinquennial congresses and of implementing some of their decisions. The committee formulates guidelines for crime prevention and criminal justice, elaborates standards and norms for the administration of criminal justice, and designs prototype agreements in addition to other relevant instruments which are then submitted to the congresses for adoption. The committee also elaborates proposals to various United Nations bodies and congresses about international cooperation and coordination of all crime-related activities. The committee periodically acts as an oversight committee to other crime programs within the United Nations. The committee was instrumental in establishing and developing the United Nations Institute on Crime Prevention and Criminal Justice.

U.N. Criminal Justice Information Network

The application of computer technology as an integral part of crime prevention and criminal justice systems should be considered an essential in obtaining success of crime prevention efforts.   Sophisticated technology, including electronic information processing, should be used to meet the increasing, complex needs in a fight against crime. Therefore, exchanges of information between governments on criminal justice matters and communication among policy makers, scholars, experts, and research institutions are being developed by the network.

The School of Criminal Justice at the State University of New York in Albany cooperated in establishing an information network. Currently, the United Nations Secretary-General strives to establish a global crime prevention and criminal justice information network. The Branch would act as the central point for other United Nations institutes in collecting data from non-governmental organizations and scientific institutions.

The Eighth Congress

The Eighth United Nations Congress on the Prevention of Crime and the Treatment of Offenders occurred from August 27 to September 7, 1990; it was hosted by the Cuban government. As has been the case for recent congresses, the

Eighth was preceded by a number of preparatory interregional and regional meetings. These preparatory meetings serve to draft technical proposals and to bring them to the attention of governments at least a year before the actual congress. These precursory meetings assist in reformulating proposed recommendations and guidelines and in creating the political atmosphere necessary to adopt these measures when the congress meets. Other crucial contributions to the refinement of recommendations and guidelines are provided at the sessions of the Committee on Crime Prevention and Control. During these sessions, government observers and committee members express their views which later become incorporated in proposed texts.

The Eighth Congress reviewed a large set of documents, including forty-five reports prepared by the United Nations and many other national papers. Ultimately, the Congress approved more texts than had all previous congresses.

Forty-five resolutions were approved, with five pertaining to model treaties. These five resolutions were intended to serve as the basis for bilateral negotiations about, inter alia, extradition, mutual assistance in criminal matters, transfer of criminal proceedings, supervision of offenders conditionally sentenced or conditionally released, and prevention of crimes against the cultural heritage of countries. The contributing countries incidentally remain grateful to the Office of International Criminal Justice for providing considerable assistance in designing the model treaty for prevention of crimes against the cultural heritage of countries. The remaining forty resolutions include but were not limited to: international cooperation, non-custodial measures, treatment of juveniles and domestic violence, the use of force and firearms, the role of prosecutors and lawyers, transfer of enforcement of penal sanctions, development of crime statistics, terrorism, and environment protection.

The Eighth Congress found that organized crime and its highly destablizing and corrupting influence on fundamental social, economic, and political institutions represent a challenge demanding accrued and more effective international cooperation. In many parts of the world, transnational criminal organizations challenge legitimate authorities by gradually seizing control of much of the economy to create a major risk for national stability and integrity. The Congress considered the fact that these groups have developed increasingly sophisticated criminal techniques which transcend present control capabilities of individual countries. As a result of an open and international kind of world, the mobility of merchandise, goods, and persons is increased while national states face difficulties in enforcing their laws. No single government can deal alone with this kind of international crime.

The Congress members hope that their adopted resolutions of a legal and semi-legal nature will provide the cooperative foundation for an international structure which will make life difficult for offenders. The resolutions aim at achieving success in the struggle against criminality by eliminating many of the loopholes in today's semi-chaotic, collaborative modality. The work of the members and the recent resolutions strive to create an international penal order, an objective that becomes particularly important when reviewing the nature and dynamics of crime. Research has demonstrated that the severity of the sanction for a given offense usually represents less of a deterrent to crime than the certainty of getting caught.

Conclusion

The Branch monitors how countries voluntarily implement the recommendations of the Eighth Congress. The recommendations, guidelines, and standards are not binding on governments. However, many countries, having agreed to the recommendations, seek the Branch's assistance in maintaining current data and in taking the necessary steps toward these written concepts of the Congress into action.

Comparison of China's Group Crime to the West's Organized Crime

by Wu Han

Organized crime has been a problem of common interest to the United Nations, to the judiciaries of many countries, and to world criminologists. It follows, therefore, that in-depth studies into its structure, its objective laws, and an examination of its social dangers should be attempted to effectively repress organized crime through intensified international efforts.

The United Nations' Secretary General stated in 1983 in his report (E/AC, 57/1986/CRP. 1, Report of the Secretary General. Part C. Article 42) on the enforcement of the U.N. Resolution on Crime Prevention that organized crime has increasingly crossed national boundaries, was often camouflaged under apparently legitimate business activity, and was extremely difficult to combat. He urged member states to increase their activity at the international level in order to combat organized crime.

The Secretary General added at the 1990 Eighth U.N. Congress on Prevention of Crime and Treatment of Offenders that "...although one of the most prominent forms of organized crime was illicit drug trafficking, there were many other forms of organized crime that might pose a threat to domestic tranquility and subvert national economics. The co-operation between some criminal organizations may be far closer than that between governments. Under the proposed topic of organized crime and terrorist activities, it would also be appropriate to deal with illegal activities, such as tax evasion and avoidance, and to seek a common solution to the problem of 'money laundering,' an activity aimed at legitimatizing illegal proceeds gained from drug-related or other large-scale offenses." (A/CONF.121/22,p66,Part E.)

He also emphasized in the resolution adopted at the Congress that national and international activities be further strengthened to deal with organized and terrorist crimes.

Why has organized crime been so rampant and reckless in different parts of the world over the years? Much of organized crime involves its social system, its political background, and its structural form. What is known internationally as organized crime is what is called in China "the crime committed by sinister societies and gangs" in old China.

Criminal societies and gangs in Chinese history were the product of feudalism from generation to generation. They became an extremely serious problem in the 1890s. Their members would stop at nothing to unlawfully monopolize, extort, blackmail, and criminally embezzle. They oppressed people, disrupted commerce, engaged in larceny and robbery, kidnapped people, and trafficked in drugs. They operated casinos or bawdy houses or drug dens, trafficked in weaponry, they murdered and abduct people. Leaders became Shanghai millionaires or celebrities. Wang Jinrong, the boss of the "Qing Gang" was made the Chinese inspector general of the police in the French Concession in Shanghai, while Chiang Kai-shek actively sought Wang's support and as a result the "Qing Gang" received the patronage of the Koumingtong (KMT) as well as the patronage of imperialist powers. The gang became more reckless and wanton in its offenses. Other leaders held important posts in the KMT army and in municipal or provincial governments. These bosses formed the gang's leadership and monopolized the gang's decision-making, giving intermediate, important positions to their "disciples" under such titles as "Director General," "General Manager," "Trustee of Chamber of Commerce." These disciples supervised various criminal activities, entrusting their underlings with specified assignments to execute particular crimes. Their underlings then recruited hooligans, hitters, killers, and other specialized criminals to commit the actual crimes.

On the eve of Shanghai's liberation, Chiang Kai-shek, the imperialists in China, and the "Qing Gang," aware of their imminent end, left the mainland for Taiwan and eventually became founding fathers of the "Bamboo Gang," "Pine League," and "Tiandao League" on Taiwan and the "Triade," "14K" and "Suihuang" in Hong Kong and Macao. Those who remained on the mainland were arrested by law enforcement agencies and given harsh sentences.

The "Qing Gang" had for several decades been committing major crimes; it was totally liquidated on the mainland after the founding of the People's Republic of China, but its members have resumed their criminal activities on Taiwan after Liberation and have extended them with organized crime in the West.

Currently, public security and public order in China are basically good. Politicians, jurists, and tourists from overseas have a sense of security in the PRC. However, in spite of some fluctuation over the years, the national crime rate in China is increasing. Recently, group or collective crimes have increased, but they are different from the crimes of the "Qing Gang."

In China, group crime occurs when a criminal, unable to consummate a certain crime alone, resorts to a group of accomplices. As a result, a crime group is loosely formed without any permanent membership and is automatically disbanded the moment the crime had been committed. The crime is a case of joint offense under the Chinese criminal law. Often, someone from one group after its automatic disorganization joins another group. When the group again is dissolved, the criminal will drift to find another group.

In addition to group crime, crime collectives have been identified in China. A crime collective is a criminal organization with a policy-making chief in command, a relatively fixed membership, and an implied "division of work" among its members. A crime collective is usually developed from a criminal group, is engaged in one kind of crime, is limited to small-scale, fixed activities, and is structurally unsophisticated.

Although organized crime is committed with political and social protection, group crime in China today is committed by two or three criminals who become targets of law enforcement.

At the top and in the core of organized crime are major investors, executives, or other well known people involved in local legislatures and generally well connected with criminal justice officials. Because of their socio-political status and lack of direct involvement in criminal activities, they have nothing to fear; the police, though well aware of them, can do nothing about them without hard evidence. Political protection covers not only the crime bosses but also their underlings, and allows organized crime to intensify its expansion. Group crime in China, however, has no political protection. Because of China's nature, the socio-political system, the Communist and other parties, the central and local people's governments, criminal justice agencies, and social organizations criminals cannot possibly be protected. Group crime leaders, having no social, political or economical status, have no access to any protection and are sure to be strictly punished once they are exposed. Group crime in China is always the invariable target of strong, concentrated attacks by law enforcement, and groups are therefore short-lived.

Structurally, organized crime is manipulated by an absolutely authoritative policy-maker for a closed organization with specialized divisions of labor among its multi-tiered membership. When a certain crime is to be committed those at the middle tier will make plans, organize activities, and assign jobs to the isolated underlings at the lowest tier. The crime will be facilitated by modern means of communication, but most underlings will not know everything about the whole execution of the crime. When a criminal case is exposed, criminals are arrested by the police. The habitual and lethal criminal of organized crime, afraid of the discipline of their organization will refuse to reveal anything. Under the circumstances, the police can only set him free for lack of hard evidence.

Because of its loose organization, the group crime members in China know each other very well and usually have committed crimes together. When one of them is caught, a lack of political protection, a policy of leniency for frank confession and a stiff sentence for refusal to cooperate often produces confessions. As a result, police can arrest the entire group immediately.

Organized crime is a kind of enterprise crime or multi-crime; group crimes in China are mostly mono-crimes, group crime seldom involves multi-crimes.

Organized crimes in the West seem to include robberies of valuables, bank hold-ups, larceny of artifacts in museums or galleries, kidnapping, hijacking, and murder. Organized crime may not include these crimes, but none of these single crimes can be isolated, and no enterprise crime can be cleared by the police to destroy the organized crime organization. In group crime in China, the crime is generally limited to one kind of activity: a high-rise house-breaking, the theft of precious metal, economic fraud, or train theft or robbery. Because the criminals are weakly organized and their offenses are limited to one kind of crime, their modus operandi is simple, and their field of action very limited. They are therefore easily detected and exposed. Many a number are caught while they are planning their crimes.

With their security and self-protection network, organized crime can use a variety of front organizations or establishments, such as factories, mills, businesses, hotels, restaurants, bars, theaters, amusement parks, and villas where the criminals can hide. Organized crime also has the benefit of its own small armed forces. When crimes fail, the criminals can easily flee the country with fake passports. Criminals involved in group crimes in China are indigent and have no protective cover or hideouts. Group criminals in China can only mix with ordinary people. They may have some illegal gains, but as strangers among local people, they cannot remain at large for long. Rather, they can easily be identified by their appearance, and the police can be informed about their whereabouts. Chinese society is a highly organized one, and the criminal stranger is doomed to be identified and arrested.

In law enforcement and criminal justice, no effective countermeasures have been found in the West to fight organized crimes. The Seventh United Nations Congress on the Prevention of Crime and the Treatment of Offenders listed the following three major crimes in the world today: drug-trafficking, terrorism, and organized crimes. Organized crime seems to be involved in those first two crimes. Organized crimes are very difficult for law enforcement which is very restricted and handicapped by statutory limitations. The top leaders of organized crime are within the surveillance of the police who are, however, paralysed by legislative technicalities. Organized criminals seem afraid of the police, and the police seem afraid of the organized criminals. Hampered in their fight against organized crime by legal technicalities, the police become easy victims to organized criminals who assassinate them or frame them. It is quite understandable that, under the circumstances, the police can neither effectively protect the people nor themselves from organized crime.

In group crime in China, group members are accomplices as defined under Chinese criminal law. It is China's policy that they be the target of intensified police attack and be the recipient of harsh punishment. Law enforcement officers are free to attack them legally. Although group criminals have a sworn allegiance to each other to never betray a friend or to keep silence when questioned, they are quite aware that "once suspected, a criminal can find protection behind an iron gate, if two criminals are suspected, they may be protected by a wooden gate; if three people are suspected, they are protected behind a paper gate; if four are suspected, they are protected by no gate at all." In China, members of crime groups are psychologically not assured of protection and therefore are apt to fall into law enforcement dragnets. Police in China, however, have the support of the public, the cooperation of organizations and agencies, and a centralized command. They also work within a society with a comprehensive structure for social peace and order and with close cooperation with security forces. Therefore, crime groups are short-lived in China.

Group crime in China today is entirely different from the organized crime in the West. However, group and organized crimes might somehow become linked, and if that began, quick investigation, crackdowns, and severe sentencing would be China's response. Under no circumstances, however, will group crime develop into organized crime as such in China. Nor will organized crime, without political protection, be given a chance to seriously endanger the people and society.

The determinative in China is nothing else than the country's social and political system which no one can change or would dare violate.

Finally, China is alert in watching any potential transnational and transient organized crime penetrating into China. The country, China is informed, is ready for any eventuality, and is determined to stop any attempt of organized crime from abroad.

Research Perspectives on Organized Crime

by Edwin Kube

In many countries, criminal offenders engage in professional and joint criminal activities with increasing flexibility. Transnational offenders often make use of a highly industrialized country's infrastructures such as modern transportation systems, computerized communications, and sophisticated ways to transfer goods and monies. Profits from these ventures remain extraordinarily high, and justice-related enforcement methods have not been able to keep pace with these new, innovative techniques.

To meet this criminal challenge, criminologists will need to shift their focus from studying exclusively individual criminal careers to studying qualitative theories and methodologies

which are applicable to the international aspects of criminal
organizations.

Research

Research should be encouraged which stresses the
definition, extent, structure, and development of organized
crime, and to exploratory studies evaluating the effectiveness
of existing countermeasures. Good analytical research will
provide a substantive basis for prevention programs.

Whether and to what extent organized crime exists in a
certain country depends primarily on the definition one
employs for criminals and crime. Organized crime can be
defined in narrow or broad terms. The definition usually
changes from the officially prescribed meaning when the
terminology becomes applied to practical, everyday law
enforcement concerns.

It therefore seems advisable to include phenomenological
studies in evaluations of organized crime, because they
analyze the variations in organizations used by offenders in
certain fields of crime. It may prove revealing to explore how
organizations differ between regions and countries. One
important factor to consider in drug dealing and illegal arms
trade would be the interactions among a resident accomplice,
a depot manager, a courier, a supervising agent, a planner, and
a financial backer. An understanding of these individual's
circumstances and their subjective response to them would
furnish a good basis for evaluating measures of prevention
and repression.

Phenomenological surveys would also assist in identifying
shifts in the delinquency structure within the entire criminal
sector. They would reveal the links between the increased
automation of financial transactions and crimes involving
credit cards and checks. These surveys may provide clues
about the existence of key offenses such as the possible
connection between government corruption and certain
environmental offenses. Such considerations enable better

scientific disclosure of the interrelations which may exist between an acute waste disposal problem and an organized environmental crime. The analysis of organized crime's sociostructure, especially with regard to new economic and technical developments, holds equal importance.

Further clarification of organized crime's involvement in other markets—its illegal entry into the labor market and employment of labor personnel—would also be helpful. This involvement remains an unimportant aspect of organized crime in Western Europe now, because illegal laborers who join the labor market come from regions which have a poor infrastructure and lack a welfare system.

In addition to an economic perspective, phenomenological studies may help to determine whether certain, legally-unsatisfied market demands for such things as weapons procurement, sexual proclivities, or medication receive accommodation from markets operating illegally by organized criminals.

Questions about organized crime usually fall into two categories. First, to what extent does organized crime and corruption become linked? Research about corruption, its causes, its nature and effect, and its links to organized crime, if it exists, stands as a prerequisite for developing effective preventive and repressive, anti-corruption measures.

Second, what is the social and organizational structure of crime systems such as those employed by drug traffickers? Although drug trafficking has often been referred to as an industry, it remains doubtful that its internal units represent organized and cooperate efforts as they do in typical multi-national business corporations, such as IBM or Mercedes-Benz. To understand such illegal enterprises, consequently, it remains essential that a detailed and reliable analysis pay close attention to the cultural and political contexts of organizations when striving to provide a complete description of drug trafficking systems.

It remains noteworthy, at least in Western Europe, that disciplines outside the field of criminology rarely show any interest in organized crime. Economic studies, for instance, could contribute to a better recognition of the effects that organized crime has on legal sectors of the economy. These studies might uncover destructive competition practices. An economic study might show how crime creates a whirlpool effect by drawing legally operating enterprises into an eddy of organized crime.

Political science studies could also assist criminologists by concentrating on the degree of penetration and influence organized crime holds within political systems, and on how organized crime affects security and law enforcement policies. Two central lines of inquiry might be: To what extent does corruption exist and influence people in public office, and how does the public's attitude change over time toward government and politics?

As easy as it may be to list items of research, it remains just as difficult to offer appropriate data-collection methods. A large amount of material such as crime situation reports, investigation files, and sentencing accounts, exists for case analysis. How a person actually selects data for review presents diverse problems, because the researcher's ontology often enters into the selection process. Consequently, the problem of objectivity in and of itself represents a key problem.

Analysis of documents, however, could be supplemented with surveys by professionals who have insight about the world of crime such as police officers, judges, public prosecutors, defense attorneys, and journalists. The preferred method of face-to-face interviews could be augmented with written questionnaires. Oral and written responses may also be influenced by the interviewee's personal interests. Another avenue to pursue would be to conduct surveys with people on organized crime's periphery. Waiters working in red-light districts, taxi drivers, and employees associated with enterprises dealing in illegal proceeds could provide useful information. Observation of these people within the marginal zones of organized crime offers yet another suitable method.

Results of One Research Project

With Europe growing increasingly united, the Research and Training Institute of the BKA conducted a research project entitled, *Organized Crime—How Great Is the Danger?* (Dorman, Koch, Risch, and Vahlenkamp. *Organisierte Kriminalitat—Wie grob ist die Gefahr?* Wiesbaden, 1990) The researchers enlisted assistance from twenty-six experts working in such fields as law enforcement, justice administration, science, the media, and the business community. Relative to the new European Community, these experts commented upon organized crime's potential threat and development in the Federal Republic of Germany. All were queried about ways to intensify efforts to fight crime.

The Delphian study promised anonymity and focused on two essential issues: assessment of future trends and ways to combat organized crime. A written questionnaire with nineteen topic areas presented interviewees with questions having no definitive answers. The survey provided the opportunity to express different experiences, points of view, and impressions about crime information. The survey's intent was not to collect solid facts about organized crime, but instead the survey aimed at having experts expound about society's political, social and economic processes. The findings of the study were used in reaching rational assessments about the future development of organized crime.

Assessment of Future Trends

The experts fear that in the coming years organized crime will grow continuously both quantitatively and qualitatively. In other words, the proportion of organized crime offenses in comparison to general crime will double by the year 2000. High profits and low risk will orient more criminals toward organized crime. Increased communication between criminal groups in the East and in the West will also provide the potential to bring organized crime into the international arena. These factors will prompt foreign offenders to become more active in the Federal Republic of Germany, as they increasingly gain influence and expand their structures and illegal activities.

Assessments of these types of organized crime thus should include: the seriousness of the offense, the quality of the modus operandi, the extent of turnover within criminal structures, and the follow-up about direct and indirect concomitant delinquency such as that already evidenced in the drug sector. The seriousness of an organized criminal offense, for example, includes not only the risk level, but also its material, personal, social, and political damage. The experts foresee a high increase in the extent of this type of total damage.

Organized crime's modus operandi will increasingly reflect more professionalism. New management skills and technical know-how, as well as investment capital from individuals unlinked to crime today, will begin to flow into criminal enterprises. These developments will lead to criminal entrepreneurs offering offenders sophisticated security and camouflage mechanisms, undoubtedly enmeshed with legal support, whereby offenders will effectively allude authorities.

Drug delinquency and white collar crime, according to the experts, appear to be the main crime areas for the 1990s. As a result, the field of unreported crime will assume a new format: the emphasis will shift from petty offenses to more serious offenses.

Regionally, organized crime will continue to spread in the Federal Republic of Germany for a number of reasons. Germany comprises a promising, growth-oriented economy which maintains both stable currency levels and wide-ranging prosperity. It also contains an agreeable demographic composition and a favorable technological infrastructure.

Germany also has freedom of movement and settlement policies and an advanced degree of liberalism. The country's current productive areas of industrialization and its metropolises attract organized crime offenders. Future suburban areas, rural districts which border other European countries, and accessible travel enclaves will also gain importance for organized crime.

Organized crime operating at the international level, the survey showed, will quickly adapt to the new, changing conditions in Europe. The introduction of a single European market which abolishes border checks and promotes the unrestricted movement of goods, services, persons, and capital vividly illustrates one such condition. The unification of the two German states with their unequal market structures and the ongoing liberalization movements in East European countries present two more threatening conditions identified by the survey's experts.

These political and economic processes will encourage crime organizations to restructure and foster new types of international delinquency. Traditional types of delinquency very likely will lose ground. Seen from this perspective, organized crime stands to benefit from the positive processes occurring in Europe and from the apparent policy shortcomings hampering justice-related efforts in European states which have yet to keep pace with all of these new changes.

The opening of borders promoting free movement favors the expansion of organized crime and strengthens its international networks in two ways. Organized criminal groups become more fortified, and their activities intertwine increasingly with politico-economic areas of society. The international aspect of organized crime thus looms as a danger that will increase to the very detriment of domestic security in all countries.

Economic pressures in competition with legal mores and profit incentives will induce today's honorable businessmen to seriously consider participating in illegal transactions. The threshold preventing crime in the past will diminish. Perceived corruptive opportunities and dubious interpersonal dependencies will accelerate this downward trend. Consequently, if this problem does not become clearer than it is today to all sections of society, communities will gradually come to accept organized crime as the norm. Such publicly sanctioned viewpoints will lead to an ongoing change in social values and behavior, concomitantly nurturing a serious shift in attitude about the law and society's understanding of justice.

In the long run, a permanent loss of confidence in a society's political system, coupled to the attraction of an organized crime's profit-making system, could lead to Mafioso conditions if countermeasures are not taken in a timely fashion and in an appropriate manner. The Federal Republic of Germany does not remain immune to this possibility. One current problem the survey participants identified was the lack of legislation specifically directed at organized crime. The experts recommended that legal, tactical, and organizational measures be improved for better deployment by law enforcement authorities. They also suggested that government and social measures would be substantially aided, if the public would become more mobilized against organized crime and would endorse more strongly, justice-related efforts. This writer believes that attention to keeping the public aware of these matters has been neglected, and in the last decade of the twentieth century that they should become one of the world-wide strategies in the war on organized crime.

Ways To Combat Organized Crime

Participants in the research project listed four problem areas worth reviewing as a means to combat organized crime. First, adequate methods must be developed for police forces and other related organizations. Conspiratorial practices characterize organized crime; as a result criminal activities contain a secrecy factor. Enmeshment of legal and illegal practices adds to the difficulty of detection. The experts, however, anticipated an imminently decisive breakthrough in organized crime definition. The definition would provide a practical instrument for distinguishing organized crime from general crime. Only in this way will it be possible to develop an instrument which allows compilation of meaningful statistical data about organized crime.

The next area experts advocated for improvement concerned the legal tools available to law enforcement officials. Enhanced legal mechanisms would increase overall effectiveness. A revision of the Criminal Procedure Code would provide more evidence-gathering options. The participants refer specifically to wire-tapping, increased use of technical facilities, and enlarging the witness protection program.

Another pressing legal problem involves the need to accelerate and harmonize international legal provisions. Cross-border pursuits within a single European market suggest this need. In order to enforce legal regulations—which, in some cases, may result in drastic measures—it remains imperative that the public and law agencies reach a consensus about the necessity to implement concepts that presently lack popular support.

The survey participants identified as the third problem area that of finding an organized crime concept meaningful to practitioners working in different fields. They recommend immediate development on the national level, but preferably on an international level, of some coordinated strategies to combat organized crime. One component of this concept remains the need to establish or enforce efficient, specialized police departments mandated to concentrate daily on organized crime and to employ investigative methods now classified as unconventional.

In order to reveal organized crime, a sufficient number of professionals must be available in specialized departments. Investigations need to focus on the offenders, not the offense. Personnel must be highly motivated people who are adequately trained, skilled in tactics, and equipped with the best materials. All this requires financial backing and is the only possible way, and the way considered most necessary, to create enough pursuit pressure on organized criminals. Effective channels of communication should be established for the national and international exchange of information. Investigations in cases of organized crime should be supported by a computer-assisted information system and should, whenever appropriate, include other authorities involved in the fight against organized crime.

The fourth and final problem area the experts recognized was that the fight against organized crime must generally be the task of the entire society. The elaboration of a general social concept and of long-ranged coordinated measures is imperative. Such a concept should deal with, inter alia, youth unemployment, unfavorable social structures, societal inequities which divides populations into privileged and underprivileged groups, and questions about the public's understanding of justice and the changing mores in societal values.

One noticeable sign of change, according to the experts, is how organized criminals penetrate social structures by placing their own people into legitimate, social, and political enterprises. A prerequisite for close cooperation between social institutions, therefore, would be to make the public more aware of this fact and the inherent dangers of how organized crime manifests itself. Awareness of these problems could be approached by utilizing trustworthy journalists and other representatives of the mass media in carefully directed and efficient public relations efforts. The project's objective would be to engender public confidence in the work done by responsible government authorities.

The survey experts add to the preparation of such concerted action the need for criminological research aimed at improving how organized crime is examined, and how to best develop the means of prevention and suppression. Research which evaluates combat measures employed by police units would also be a component of this undertaking.

A Preventive Approach

In the field of organized crime, both conspicuous offenders and clandestine backers exercise rational business acumen under the guise of seizing maximum profit. Their various bases of operation—the logistic element—depend on their branch of crime or business.

In cases of drug-related crime, laboratory expertise and equipment represent the first essentials for successful drug production, whereas the marketing arm of drug trafficking concentrates on creating transport and depot systems and distribution networks. In cases of investment fraud, offenders seek first to establish solid company reputations and then work on recruiting eloquent sales staff. In cases of racketeering, organized criminals solicit operatives who are both willing to commit and have the requisite skills for violence. In other crime cases, procurement, employment, and maintenance of special technical equipment, such as scanners used in forgery, become the necessary prerequisites.

One observation can be made for all these types of offenses: money represents the motivating factor in the planning and commission of organized crime. This observation becomes especially evident in light of the growing tendency among criminals to invest large sums to secure know-how or acquire connections to high-ranking figures such as politicians or government officials. Establishing and maintaining cooperation by employing corrupt practices with high-ranking figures in government, business, politics, and within justice-related agencies, characterize one organized crime method. External advisors also are frequently brought on the payroll, and organized crime groups maintain a welfare system for those on their payroll. They grant legal representation to offenders who are caught and provide financial security to convicts and their defendants.

Attempts to eradicate or obstruct the logistic element of organized crime represent a new preventive approach. It begins with research about the dimension and structure of criminal logistics. This research includes three categories: procurement, organizational structure, and distribution.

Logistical procurement strategies involve the recruitment of suitable personnel to gain information and the corruption of people holding public office. They also entail acquiring materials for commission of a crime and later providing cover to organizational members.

One result of research may be to show that access to instruments and objects used in various branches of organized crime need to be subjected to more stringent controls than in the past. This approach would be difficult. While such materials represent a criminal's tools-of-the-trade, the materials themselves remain socially neutral, because placing restrictions on such items as computers would affect criminals and citizens alike. One positive development in this undertaking, however, has been the measures aimed at preventing multi-purpose industrial chemicals from being funneled into channels where they might be used to produce illegal narcotics. The Association of the Chemical Industry in Germany instituted a self supervised system to intensify the controls over such substances. Chemicals, which might be used in the refinement and production of illegal drugs, are classified on a warning list, and the list is updated at regular intervals. These classified chemicals may only be delivered to dealers and refiners who are able to provide checkable declarations on the final recipient. These regulations generally comply with provisions established by the United Nations and the European Community.

Another logistical consideration in which law enforcement agencies need to direct their energies pertains to the internal structure of criminal organizations. The focus could be on forfeiting criminal proceeds and penetrating compartmentalized structures. Nowadays, there can be no doubt that all suitable means of intervention should be concentrated and used to undermine the financial logistic backbone of organized crime. One way to do this would be to employ stringent controls on international money transfers. Organized crime proceeds that are transferred many times through international banking systems should be prevented from receiving asylum.

One approach for cracking a compartmentalized structure would be to break down any community of trust in the criminal scene. This approach would not only include classic tactical measures, such as undercover investigations or raids but also, as in Germany, the introduction of state's evidence. Other strategies include infiltrating organized crime's data systems prior to the information reaching the chosen targets. Disseminating information to the public would be beneficial if gained in this manner or if it was acquired by successful police action. Naturally, all of these strategies must take into account the consequences of such action relative to legal and socio-ethical considerations.

Finally, distribution logistics also offer a very promising, preventive approach to organized crime. Law enforcement services employ specific strategies in this area in their development of suspect data. The Bundeskriminalamt, for instance, employs the so-called container Program to counter illicit drug trade. Their container project was a response to organized crime's use of freight containers for smuggling. Such a container was easy to build, provided a good way to store and conceal drugs, and its quick handling and high traffic volume had advantages for both sender and recipient. The Bundeskriminalamt group, therefore, now conducts computer-aided checks on container traffic data based on a catalog of selective criteria. Suspected containers are checked with the aid of drug detection devices in the country of transit or destination.

Effective Legal Prevention Measures

If the experts' forecasts are valid about the quantitative and qualitative aggravation of organized crime, it remains imperative that law enforcement agencies work on intensive prevention, especially in the area of logistics. Other preventive and repressive measures, of course, should not be neglected.

Current conditions in Western Europe and elsewhere find police and judicial authorities employing classic law enforcement measures to organized crime, and this course of action results in limited prevention.

Only the consequent implementation of all types of prevention measures will assist in winning the battle in what may be a partially lost war against organized crime. Whether or not this war can be actually won will depend upon how organized crime research contributes successfully to practical law enforcement work. Obtaining good research data depends upon the degree of international cooperation and interdisciplinary efforts, which supports and encourages criminologists in their quest for knowledge.

The Crime Prevention Mission of the Postal Inspection Service

by Michael Ahern

Crimes against individuals are traumatic. Enterprise crimes include crimes against individuals, groups of people, and entire societies. These crimes wreak havoc on entire communities, industries, and businesses while tearing at the fabric of our societies. Although a country's procedures to prevent these crimes may differ, all law officials remain bascially concerned for the security of populations and property. Enforcement officers also share the basic elements of investigation and apprehension towards those who practice criminal activities.

The Postal Inspection Service, which represents the law enforcement and investigative branch of the United States

Postal Service, embraces these concerns. Fundamentally, a crime against the United States postal service is a federal offense. A postal inspector, therefore, represents a federal law enforcement agent who has police authority, carries a weapon, and makes arrests. Shunning publicity, postal inspectors for many years were referred to as the "Silent Service." Today postal inspectors, eager to let people know their proud history, publicize their ongoing efforts to protect the United States mails, postal personnel, property, and customers. As the oldest federal law enforcement organization in the United States, the Postal Inspection Service represents a historic organization in the modern world.

History of the U.S. Postal Service

From the days of horse-carried mail to today's miracles in technology, an integral component of the inspection service has always been to service the needs of the entire country. Benjamin Franklin, appointed postmaster at Philadelphia in 1737, stated his duties included regulating post offices and bringing the postmasters to account. Franklin's other assigned duties were similar in scope to many duties assumed by today's postal inspectors. In the eighteenth century postal inspectors were called surveyors, and they visited post offices, arrested thieves and robbers, assisted in improving methods of transportation, and helped to establish post offices.

As the postal service system expanded, so did the responsibilities of the inspectors. United States history frequently reflects their innumerable contributions. Postal inspectors expedited mail to military personnel during the Spanish-American War. When gold was discovered in the Yukon, inspectors established post offices in the new towns being founded in the wilderness, appointed postmasters, and hired contractors to deliver the mail. Inspectors also solved the first known stagecoach robbery in which the driver was killed and more than $3,000 was stolen from the mail. The bandits were caught within five days. Another famous investigation involved two historic American characters, Butch Cassidy and the Sundance Kid. While fleeing from several horsemen, one asked the other, "Who are those guys?" The other responded, "Postal Inspectors."

The second and third decades of the twentieth century were eras of lawlessness in the United States. Gangs robbed banks, post offices, and trains with increasing frequency. Robberies of mail trains became a new challenge to the postal system. The great gold holdup by three brothers in 1923 took postal inspectors to Canada, Mexico, Europe, and South America for more than three years. The brothers were eventually caught, convicted, and sentenced to life imprisonment.

Crime solving followed a standard pattern in all of these episodes. A crime was committed; inspectors investigated; offenders were identified, arrested, and prosecuted. Inspectors continually recommended security measures to correct weaknesses in the postal system, and their recommendations remain important today, although modern times demand modern techniques.

Composition of the Postal Service

The inspection service maintains 149 field offices in the United States, including five regional headquarters and five crime laboratories. Investigative resources reside within thirty-nine divisions. A division head reports to a regional chief inspector, who reports directly to the chief postal inspector in Washington, D. C. Nationwide, the inspection service consists of nearly 2,000 postal inspectors, 1,600 uniformed security officers, and 800 support staff. The inspection service also includes among its ranks, attorneys, certified public accountants, and others holding advanced degrees in numerous fields.

A person must be a college graduate to be a postal inspector today. Other requirements include passing a written examination, undergoing a complete background investigation and medical examination, performing successfully during an assessment center process, and completing twelve-weeks of intensive training at the postal service management academy in Potomac, Maryland. Any interested professionals who intend to travel to the Washington, D. C. area may visit the postal service training facility.

The inspection service's five regional crime laboratories provide expert support to postal personnel. The laboratories have kept pace with technological advances in such areas as document analysis, forensic photography, chemistry, physical evidence, and fingerprint identification.

Computerization enables the inspection service to communicate with other law enforcement agencies in the country. Computers are also employed to analyze crime trends and investigative leads. All postal facilities have state-of-the-art security equipment.

Several years ago, the inspection service realized that identification, detection, investigation, and subsequent conviction of those violating postal laws was insufficient. The responsibility of the service also included preventing crime and providing assistance in educating the American public about types of mail fraud. A prevention program was initiated to anticipate, identify, and analyze those areas of great crime risk and to take measures to maintain the integrity of the mails. The inspection service conducts seminars and provides public service announcements and publications which suggest how to avoid being victimized and what to do if it happens. Inspection service personnel also participate in radio and television interviews to discuss victimization and to preserve the integrity of the United States mail.

However, inspection service efforts are specifically directed at preventing postal crimes by providing education programs and by taking security measures, monitoring mail services by conducting a strong internal audit program, and investigating crimes against the service and its postal customers. Just as it did some two hundred years ago, today's postal inspection service investigates violations of postal laws. Postal statutory authority includes carrying firearms, serving subpoenas and warrants, and making arrests. Postal inspectors are still responsible for protecting the United States mail, postal employees, postal property, and postal customers against crime. Postal inspectors, however, are not responsible for any private carriers, such as the United Postal Service (UPS) or Federal Express.

When one considers that the United States Postal Service employs almost 800,000 people, processes and delivers mail daily to more than 117 million addresses in the nation, including rural and urban areas, the immensity and complexity of its task becomes apparent. The postal service also delivers daily a half a billion dollars in negotiable goods, other tangible valuables, and irreplaceable items of inestimable value.

Investigative Responsibilities

Criminal investigative responsibilities are classified into four broad categories. The first, external crimes, includes mail theft, robberies and burglaries against postal facilities, and assaults upon postal personnel. The second, internal crimes, includes theft of mail and postal property and misappropriation of postal funds by postal employees. Mail fraud crime, the third category, involves the victimization of postal customers by the fraudulent use of the United States Postal System and United States Mail. The fourth category includes prohibited mailings. United States laws prohibit the mailing of illegal narcotics, hazardous materials such as bombs, and child pornography. The inspection service investigates, arrests, and assists in preparing evidence for the trials and convictions of people who attempt to mail prohibited items.

The inspection service also remains responsible for internal audits. Such internal financial audits supplement annual external audits completed by certified public accountants.

Other operational, developmental, and contract audits serve to make the postal service efficient, economical, and reliable.

Mail Crime Statistics

From October 1989 to October 1990, mail theft by non-employees led to 4,742 arrests and 3,798 convictions. Postal robbery investigations and burglary resulted in 377 arrests and 313 convictions. Approxmitately 2,000 employees were identified as participants in mail theft and other mail crimes, including sabotage of equipment and theft of postal service property. Fraud alone produced forty arrests and thirty-one convictions. From October 1990 to April 1991, postal inspectors made 6,324 arrests for postal-related crime. Inspectors issued 477 audit reports in financial, operational, and developmental areas. Millions of dollars and tens of thousands of consumer-victims were involved in these crimes.

Frequently, inspection responsibilities extend beyond state and national boundaries to assume an international dimension. In mail fraud, the mails are used to further a scheme to defraud. The terms—"use of the mails," "in furtherance of," and "scheme to defraud"—have appeared in numerous United States Appellate Court decisions. The use of the United States mails—rather than any private organization—remains an essential element in mail fraud and must include an intentional, material misrepresentation or omission of fact. All of those misuses of the mail must be proven in order to sustain a conviction of mail fraud.

Mail fraud in not new. Article I, Section 8 of the United States Constitution gave Congress enumerated powers to establish post offices and post roads and to make all necessary laws for executing its powers. After the Civil War, snake oil salesmen began using the mail service as a lucrative and less tiring way to distribute their wares. After a rash of mail order and land fraud swindles in 1872, the United States Congress enacted mail fraud statutes to supplement constitutional provisions. Medicine men and con artists, prior to 1872, had used with impunity the mails to defraud people. The West was still being settled, and mail was the primary means of communication. Most fraudulent schemes relied heavily on the use of the mail service, and local law enforcement officials lacked jurisdiction over distant swindlers.

Modern travel, telephones, and computer technology necessitate additional mail fraud statutes. Postal inspector work now includes investigating credit card, wire, and computer fraud and investigating money laundering schemes. Recent laws and age-old statutes provide the best prescriptive weapons against con artists.

The Clifford Irving case in the 1970s provides a recent illustration of mail fraud. Irving gained notoriety with his claim that he had been given the exclusive rights to write a biography of Howard Hughes, an eccentric multimillionaire. Irving devised a scheme to defraud two publishing companies of thousands of dollars, and he conducted much of the scam through the mail. The case was solved by postal inspectors with the assistance of document examiners in the postal service crime laboratory. They analyzed evidence which proved instrumental in Irving's trial and ultimate conviction. The conviction resulted after inspectors made many trips abroad to track Irving's whereabouts.

Telemarketing (or boiler room operations) became the predominate fraud in the 1980s. Civil statutes aimed at consumer protection were essential in this type of criminal investigation. Violators are punished and required to make restitution. Although telemarketing sales are not illegal, the manner in which the sales are effected concern postal inspectors. Consumers are warned not to be fooled by sophisticated telephone voices or legitimate-sounding addresses, because both may be part of a scheme to defraud. Classic elements in an illegal telemarketing sales pitch include a high pressure sales approach, an announcement of an imminent price increase, an urgency for the purchaser to make an immediate decision, an inducement to place an order, a material misrepresentation of the price and value of an item, and a fictitious high cost to the company.

Consumers confront these same elements when they buy a car or house; however, there is a difference. When a person purchases a car or house, the merchandise is seen; one can kick tires or flush a toilet. In telemarketing transactions, the customer does not see the item. Furthermore, a customer can be fooled by an inducement such as a VCR or a necklace. The inducement, euphemistically termed a premium, is in fact a bribe. The telemarketing procurement officer who offers this sort of bribe often creates excessive expense for the company and will eventually be deprived of employment.

Recently inspectors executed a search warrant at an operation on Long Island, New York. Besides gross misrepresentations and overcharging for products, the promoters bribed customers with premiums. The value of the premium was determined by the projected size of the customber's order. The premium was mailed to the customer's residence by certified mail which requires an acknowledgment of receipt. Later, the customer received a follow-up telephone call from the salesperson offering to sell more merchandise to justify the premium. When the customer hesitated to place an additional order, the salesperson quickly reminded the customer of the initial premium and the return receipt the company had on file. Some companies have "boiler room" operations in several United States cities, and they involve millions and millions of dollars.

Postal Service Remedies

The postal service employs both civil and legal methods to combat mail fraud. Depending upon the severity and type of the crime, these methods may be used individually or together. The civil or administrative remedies are oriented toward consumer protection.

In some cases, the postal service seeks voluntary discontinuance of a practice by eliciting a written promise by a promoter to cease questionable business practices. No formal hearing is held; no court action is taken; and the practice is not legally enforceable.

False representation does lead to court hearings. Anyone who receives money or property through the mail based on misrepresentation can be subjected to legal action, and it does not need to be shown that the promoter intended to defraud. Orders are issued by the judicial officer of the postal service after a formal hearing and result in the return of the promoter's mail to its sender. A cease and desist order, at the same time, prohibits the promoter from engaging in similar violations. A violation of a cease and desist order may result in civil rights fines of ten thousand dollars per day.

A third remedy involves a temporary restraining order and is sought in those cases in which consumers need special protection. The postal service must show a federal district court judge that a case of probable cause exists. It must demonstrate that the promoter has been engaging in a violation of the false representation statute and that the postal service plans to seek a false representation order. A temporary restraining order commands the postal service to detain the promoter's mail, pending the outcome of the administrative process.

To those engaged in business by mail, the mail is the life-line of a business. If their mail is detained by one of these remedies, businesses often must close. The law pertaining to mail fraud, consequently, provides a powerful weapon to the postal inspection service.

Civil administrative actions are geared towards consumer protection, but criminal prosecutions by the postal service are designed to punish violators and sometimes to seek restitution. Before lodging a criminal complaint, inspectors, like law enforcement agents, investigate complaints, tips, or information. As part of the investigation, grand jury subpoenas may be obtained to compel testimony from individuals or to obtain needed evidence. Search warrants are also particularly serviceable in "boiler room" cases and other cases involving fraud.

A federal grand jury, composed of citizens from the community, receives the investigative evidence. If they determine probable cause that a crime was committed, the jury issues a mail fraud indictment and an arrest warrant. The subject is arrested for trial, or plea bargaining may result in an agreement. Convictions result in imprisonment, fines, or restitution.

There has been a perception in the United States that punishments for white collar crime are slight. However, recently enacted sentencing guidelines include significant prison sentences and substantial fines. For example, an inspector reported a fraud sentence to his chief postal inspector as follows:

> Michael A. Smith and Ronald A. Smith were sentenced to ten years in custody, followed by five years probation. The sentence, based on ten counts of mail fraud, resulted from the Smiths' illegal operation of Crandall Financial Corporation. Crandall Financial had sold investors substantially overvalued gem stones eventuating in significant losses for approximately two thousand investors.

Ten years in prison hardly represents an easy sentence.

The recent, stringent sentencing guidelines have been employed by the inspection service in some well-known cases. In 1985, E. F. Hutton employed more than four hundred banks to transfer customer funds from one bank account to another. By taking advantage of the time required for checks to clear, E.F. Hutton had daily access to over $250 million of interest-free money. The company pleaded guilty and paid two million dollars in restitution to the postal inspection service and eight million dollars to the victimized banks.

The inspection service was responsible for identifying Ivan Boesky's stock trading scam on Wall Street. Boesky, a major stock broker, defrauded customers of more than $100 million. His arrest and eventual conviction led to identifying, arresting, and convicting a number of others who abused the use of the United States mails. Some observers feel that as a result of these investigations, Wall Street has changed the way it does business.

As a televangelist, Jim Bakker entreated millions of television viewers to send checks in the mail for time shares in his theme park, which could not possibly accommodate all those who bought time-shares. Convicted of mail fraud and sentenced to forty-five years in prison, Bakker strives to appeal the judgment.

Peter Voss was an ex-postal service governor whom postal inspectors identified as an embezzler of United States property and who accepted thousands of kickbacks from postal contractors. Voss was convicted, but the Voss case represents how many government agencies become involved in investigating fraud cases. While the inspection service remains an integral part of the United States Postal Service, it maintains rights and duties to independently investigate questions of integrity within the highest levels of the postal service. The chief postal inspector, in his capacity as inspector general of the postal service, is mandated to present a semiannual report to the United States Congress. While civil, criminal, administrative, audit and security investigations continue to be performed by all branches of the United States government, the postal service remains unique in that it is the only government entity to house all these investigations within one organization.

The International Scene

Modern technology brings countries close together, and postal inspection workers cooperate with international law enforcement communities. In 1991, Chief Postal Inspector Charles R. Clauson created the position of Assistant Chief Postal Inspector-International.

International mail fraud may involve the escape of a fugitive to another country. The inspection service continues its search for Thomas Billman, a former executive of a savings and loan association in Bethesda, Maryland. Billman, a fugitive from justice since 1988, is believed to be somewhere in Europe. He fled the United States to avoid a $112 million civil judgment against him. He is also sought in connection with a twenty count indictment charging him with defrauding savings and loan depositors of over $106 million. A $200,000 reward has been offered for his arrest; half the award is funded by the Maryland Deposit Insurance Fund, and the remainder is funded by the United States Postal Inspection Service.

Felix Kolbovsky, a Russian immigrant, boarded a plane to his homeland in January 1991, for what he believed would be a flight to freedom. He left behind a twenty-one count indictment for mail fraud. Federal charges were made against him and his sister in August 1990. The alleged charges included the use of the United States mail to defraud insurance companies by submitting company bills for unwarranted medical examinations. Kolbovsky operated four medical companies: a health care clinic and three firms that provided advanced diagnostic tests to the clinic's patients. Kolbovsky employed personnel to solicit clients by telephone and by visits to health clubs and retirement homes. False billings were later prepared and mailed to insurance companies. It is estimated that Kolbovsky's fraud represents over more than ten million dollars. The postal inspection service worked with Interpol and its member countries, including the Soviet Union, to arrange for Kolbovsky's return to the United States. The successful international effort resulted in Kolbovsky being returned to St. Louis, Missouri in March 1991 for trial.

In 1989 this writer became actively involved in an international mail fraud case when a United States Attorney in Los Angeles received a request to investigate an alleged fraud in which students in Beijing, China lost approximately seventy thousand dollars. The Douglas Catholic Fundamental Center in Los Angeles had offered assistance to students studying at Beijing's Furen Foreign Language University by providing work and student visas in exchange for approximately $1,500 in United States currency. After the students wired the money, they received no further communications from Douglas's representatives. Fifty students lost a total of $70,000. For each Chinese student, the loss represented two years of wages.

All of the mailings and wire transfers were handled by the Dean of Students at the Furen Foreign Language University. The Dean plans to come to the United States to testify that Douglas's agents designated him as their representative by furnishing him with a consignment agreement to process bogus requests. The consignment agreement was accompanied by a student agreement stating that each student would be charged an established amount for Douglas's complete line of services. The agreement would theoretically enable a student to enter the United States. In September 1989, four money-wire transfers totalling $69,000 were wired from Beijing, via the Bank of China, to a student account at Douglas Catholic Fundamental Center. During the three-month interval prior to bringing suit, Douglas representatives failed to contact the Dean despite the Dean's repeated mail and telephone requests.

Postal inspectors investigated the Douglas money transfer scheme, and their analysis revealed aspects of money-laundering and two additional fraudulent activities. One connivance, which appeared to be operating concurrently with the Douglas case, involved a second group of Chinese students victimized in a similar fashion. A second scheme involved an apparently fictitious company, Shell Investors and Labor Institute, which promised jobs to Chinese students for a finder's fee of $1,000.

The mission of the inspection service was stated succinctly by a United States District Judge during an issuance of a preliminary injunction in a mail fraud case:

> The American people have come to respect the postal service and expect that its integrity shall at all times be maintained, and for anyone to misuse the institution of the postal service, to misuse the United States mail, is very repugnant and intolerable....The government has an obligation to make sure that the mails are not used to deceive the American people through improper and false solicitations [and] that the obligation of the government becomes even greater as the mobility of the American people increases and the population increases....[The postal service is to be commended] for its vigilance in undertaking this prompt investigation.

The postal inspection service also remains dedicated to ensuring that the United States mails are not used to deceive people from other countries. It refuses to carry items prohibited in the United States to other nations or to deliver compensation derived from illegal activities, and it works to uncover money laundering endeavors. The postal inspection service wants to take the profit out of crime, and it works with law enforcement organizations nationally and internationally to unify strategies and practices.

Crime Commissions and the War against Enterprise Crime

by Fredrick T. Martens

Enterprise crime, a rather new criminological phenomenon, traces its roots to what was commonly referred to as organized crime. By its uniqueness, enterprise crime often requires extraordinary investigative techniques and remedies. Electronic surveillance, witness immunity, criminal and civil forfeiture, and the Racketeer Influenced Corrupt Organizations Act (RICO) become part of the so-called arsenal available to attack enterprise crime.

This arsenal of remedies responds to enterprise crime from a criminal or civil perspective, but prosecution is the ultimate goal. However, by focusing exclusively on making a case, law enforcement may overlook the nuances characterizing an enterprise crime business and may not take other preventive remedies that may be cost-efficient and effective.

Developing a regulatory system to expose and prohibit the immigration of racketeers may be far more effective and cost efficient than responding to them later. Liquor establishments, construction companies, and the casino industry can also be regulated. Certainly, organized crime would be more susceptible to opportunity-blocking regulations than to criminal prosecution. Publicly-funded crime commissions can be a relatively inexpensive response to the chronic problem of enterprise crime.

Topologies

Essentially three kinds of crime commissions exist in the United States. First, publicly-funded crime commissions often derive their powers from individual state legislatures. These commissions are given law enforcement status and concomitant authority with the exception of arrest and prosecution powers. The New Jersey, New York, and Pennsylvania Crime Commissions have this status. Bi-partisan in composition, commission members are appointed by both political parties, thereby promoting the independent status of the commissions, with no political party having exclusive control. Supported by tax revenues, a commission's budget remains relatively modest in comparison to other groups within the criminal justice system.

A second kind of crime commission involves citizen groups usually funded by private contributions from the business community. A citizens' crime commission has no law enforcement authority. The legendary Chicago Crime Commission headed by the infamous Virgil Petersen, the Citizens' Crime Commission in New York, and the Citizens' Crime Commission of the Greater Delaware Valley in Pennsylvania characterize this kind of commission.

The third kind of crime commission consists of a temporary group who have been legislated or enacted by executive order to investigate after the fact a specific incident, event, or phenomenon. The Lilley Commission, charged with the investigation of the Newark riots in 1967, derived its authority from an executive order by former New Jersey Governor Richard Hughes. It was funded by public revenues, had subpoena powers, and could hold both public or private hearings. President Lyndon B. Johnson's executive order created the Kerner Commission in 1968 to investigate the causes of civil disorder in the United States. It, like President Ronald Reagan's 1983 Commission on Organized Crime, was publicly-funded, had subpoena power, and could hold both public and private hearings. Once a commission's goal has been achieved or the commission's time period for action has expired, the commission is terminated. Those kinds of commissions are analogous to Royal Commissions in Hong Kong, Japan, Great Britain, and Australia.

All three commissions serve to educate and mobilize the public, are enacted to address a specific phenomenon, and do not necessarily collect evidence of criminal activity. However, they are not precluded from providing criminal evidence to law enforcement authorities. The following comments relate to publicly-funded crime commissions such as the Pennsylvania Crime Commission.

A Legal Anomaly

United States laws are classified as criminal, civil, and administrative; each requires a different standard of proof. Criminal law requires proof beyond a reasonable doubt, and the rules of evidence are exact and restrictive. Civil law applies a preponderance-of-the-evidence standard, and evidential rules are liberal. Administrative law usually deals with regulatory matters; it relies upon a standard of reasonable inference which may be obtained from secondary sources.

Criminal punishment varies as well. In a criminal conviction, death or loss of a person's freedom for a considerable period of time may be imposed. In a civil judgment, usually financial remuneration is exacted. An administrative violation may carry a penalty of a suspension of a license or a contract dismissal. Punishments are graduated, as are a penalty's standards of proof. Moreover, intent becomes more of a critical factor in a criminal case than in civil or administrative hearings.

Crime commissions such as those in Pennsylvania, New Jersey, and New York have been specifically mandated to expose organized crime and other kinds of public corruption. Their mandates to expose do not include proof beyond a reasonable doubt. Their mandates rely upon a standard of proof which allows a commission to draw reasonable inferences from all the evidence, information, and testimony it collects and examines. This expansive standard of proof allows crime commissions to expose (vis-a-vis prosecute) conditions and individuals far more than traditional law enforcement agencies do under the law.

The Pennsylvania Crime Commission investigated and exposed racketeering in the state's solid waste industry. It gathered information and elicited testimony to demonstrate that New York and New Jersey organized crime groups had invested in Pennsylvania waste corporations. The groups' historic pattern of infiltration suggested that their racketeering and their entry into illegal waste disposal would occur. The commission recommended regulations to inhibit and prevent such activity from occurring. It also provided information to federal authorities to develop criminal prosecutions or civil judgments.

The kind of approach used in Pennsylvania to the enterprise crime problem allows a crime commission to facilitate, prod, and encourage a criminal or civil response by an appropriate law enforcement or regulatory agency. Unrestrained by traditional enterprise crime responses, a crime commission may expose a problem (vis-a-vis arresting individuals) and offer a wide array of remedial options beyond simply working towards a criminal prosecution. A crime commission, employing its law enforcement powers, can collect information and evidence and use both in either a cooperative or an adversative setting. A commission's power becomes far more inclusive and responsive to an organized crime problem than that of law enforcement. That power explains why a crime commission remains a legal anomaly; arrest and prosecution are seen as secondary to a commission's primary role of public exposure.

Other anomalies exist. A witness immunized by the New Jersey Crime Commission of Investigation can be held in contempt for a refusal to testify. Civil incarceration can result until a recalcitrant witness agrees to testify. The late Angelo Bruno was incarcerated for two-and-half years for failing to testify before the New Jersey State Commission of Investigation.

Another anomaly involves subpoenaing witnesses, a legal right granted only to crime commissions and grand juries. A subpoenaed witness must appear before a crime commission or grand jury and give testimony. The witness has the right to legal counsel and may exercise Fifth Amendment privileges against self-incrimination. The witness nonetheless must appear, and any refusal to answer questions could result in a charge of adverse inference if the information sought has already been corroborated by other witnesses. If a witness commits perjury or provides false information, that witness is subjected to further criminal sanctions, including incarceration.

A commission also holds public meetings to present its findings. Although no criminal indictment or charges are made, the public hearing serves as a forum where the commission formulates data and mobilizes public opinion to encourage institutional responses. A commission's report may be publicized to provide another means to educate the public about possible remedies. No traditional law enforcement agency in the United States has such public authority.

Libel and defamation laws cannot be extended to a crime commission, because it acts under the auspices of the legislature. Public information becomes privileged or immune from these laws. Unlike traditional law enforcement organizations which can be sued for false arrest or other civil violations, a commission is spared legal recourse from an aggrieved witness.

A Fact-Finding Commission

A legislature invests extraordinary power in a crime commission, because four assumptions exist. First, victims of organized or enterprise crime seldom complain. They are often compliant or consensual participants in criminal behavior. The prostitute who works for a john, the drug user who buys from a drug dealer, the gambler who bets with a bookmaker, or the borrower who bets money from a loan shark are all aiding and abetting criminal conduct. Demand for something illegal creates a supply. Absent extraordinary investigative techniques, most of this kind of crime occurs undetected.

Second, organized criminal methods and trade frequently nullify or compromise government action. Corruption of public officials is often employed by racketeers, but they themselves inform on competitors in the illegal marketplace. Eliminating competition becomes an essential goal of the enterprise criminal who goes beyond trading in a product or service to creating a monopoly or market superiority.

Third, violence or the threat of violence characterizes enterprise crime. Unbounded by legitimate judicial practices, criminal businesses employ their own methods for enforcing contracts or agreements. A mobster's court does impose a death sentence; however, other sentences are also imposed.

A commission's final assumption about enterprise crime recognizes that criminal acumen assists lawbreakers in eluding prosecution. Smart criminals enjoy illegally gained profits while they insulate and shield themselves from the actual criminal acts. The hierarchial nature of enterprise crime protects the well-placed corruptable government official while providing the best legal assistance to those suspected of a crime. Law enforcement agencies have recently applied RICOS to penetrate the hierarchy of enterprise crime.

The President's Commission on Law Enforcement and Administration of Justice concluded:

> States that have organized crime groups in operation should create and finance organized crime investigation commissions with independent, permanent status, with an adequate staff of investigators, and with subpoena powers. Such commissions should hold hearings and furnish periodic reports to the legislature, governor and law enforcement officials.

Combatting enterprise crime demands a well-informed public; commissions, unrestrained by traditional rules of evidence, become powerful fact-finding bodies. The bi-partisan nature of commissions alerts government and non-government agencies to enterprise crime and enlists their support to take action against criminals.

A crime commission's fact-finding, as opposed to an accusative focus, permits investigation of organized criminal operations and publication of its findings. A commission functions with the belief that real organized crime control remains a public and community responsibility. Evidence supports this belief. Although inoculating communities against the blight of enterprise crime requires eventual judicial remedies, the extent of the crime must be known. Community action ultimately remains the most effective, cost-efficient method of controlling organized crime, and crime commissions are crucial to that action.

A Civil Liberties Nightmare?

Crime commissions, by their very composition, face problems with civil liberties. Because typical rules of evidence do not apply to them and immunization from libel or defamation actions do, crime commissions may risk potential abuse. In their war against enterprise crime, crime commissions can become political or ideological battlegrounds for those who are intent on maligning or destroying an opponent's reputation or for those considered to be on the wrong side. The Pennsylvania Supreme Court stated:

> The nature of the Crime Commission calls for great circumspection in assessing the rights of citizens who may come within its investigative sweep....the magnitude of the infamy....on the mere assemblage of information untested by the fires of due process is enormous.

People in a society, knowing a crime commission can enjoin a person's freedom, place considerable trust in a crime commission's reputation for integrity. In a democracy, it appears repugnant to basic notions of due process to publicly label an individual as a racketeer, a drug dealer, or a killer without evidence to prosecute in court. However, people recognize that proof beyond a reasonable doubt is neither the same as innocence nor synonymous with non-culpability. Truth does not always surface in litigated cases and often becomes obscured. Achieving a delicate balance between a citizen's rights and the prevention of enterprise crime remains a real challenge and a struggle worth waging.

Cooperative Efforts in Combatting Drug Trafficking

by Edward J. Kelly, Jr.

On August 14, 1989, the *U.S. News and World Report* published an article entitled, "The Return of the Deadly Drug Called Horse." The article stated what the law enforcement community had known for some time: Horse, a slang word for heroin, is back on American streets. Southeast Asian syndicates trafficking in heroin now provide a more powerful and more plentiful supply than at any other time in United States history.

Drug Trafficking Statistics

Between 1985 and 1988, Kon Yu Leung, also known as Johnny Kon, a successful Shanghai-born entrepreneur, attempted to smuggle over twelve-hundred pounds of heroin into the United States. In February of 1988, Thai customs officials seized ten-hundred, eigty-six kilograms of heroin in Bangkok destined for New York. The New York office of the United States Drug Enforcement Agency investigated the case and found that the smugglers had shipped six hundred kilograms prior to the February seizure. In March of the following year, the F.B.I. seized four-hundred, twenty-five kilograms of heroin in New York. In September 1989, the Hong Kong police seized four-hundred, twenty kilograms in their city. Chinese syndicates had orchestrated all of these loads of drugs.

Why the Chinese, and why such large amounts? The answer to the latter is simple: Golden Triangle opium output quadrupled from six-hundred, twenty-five metric tons in the 1984-1985 growing season to twenty-six hundred metric tons in 1990. Parenthetically, foreign opium traders recently shipped twice this amount or fifty-six hundred metric tons into China. Today, favorable weather conditions, increased use of fertilizers, and modern planting techniques contribute to today's problem. Burma's political turmoil and its lack of effective control over opium growing areas also encourage the illegal opium industry.

In the 1960s and 1970s the mafia in France and Italy controlled the importation of heroin into the United States. Mexicans captured the heroin market in the 1970s. In the early 1980s, the Sicilian mafia tried to monopolize the market, but cooperative law enforcement efforts between the United States and Italy eliminated Sicilian involvement. Chinese syndicates then aggressively assumed control of the market; they included Sino/Myanmar growers and refiners, Thai/Chinese exporters, Hong Kong Chinese or Taiwanese brokers, Chinese/American importers and wholesalers, and Chinese underground bankers.

One common thread appears obvious. In the early 1980s, ethnic Chinese traffickers, not nationalists in the People's

Republic of China, controlled the flow of heroin from the fields to the streets. In the 1990s, Asian heroin comprises 56 percent of the United States market—this writer estimates it represents 90 percent of the New York market. The whole fabric of heroin trade and drug terminology had changed. No one speaks about drugs in terms of pounds or kilograms any longer; units or bricks sold wholesale represent a seven-hundred gram measure in Asian heroin.

Noticeable shifts in the drug's purity and price adds a further dimension to the problem. New York's office of the D.E.A. found pure street heroin, because the Chinese do not routinely adulterate their product prior to sale. Profits remain enormous. Investigations reveal that a kilogram of heroin sells for $1,200 to $1,400 in United States currency in Myanmar's Kokang region; $2,400 to $3,200 in Thailand's city of Chiang; $7,000 to $11,000 in Bangkok; and $60,000 to $20,000 in New York.

In September 1990, the D.E.A.'s New York office arrested four P.R.C. Nationalists from Guangzhou possessing duffle bags stuffed with eight million dollars from a sale of over five hundred kilograms of heroin. The case represents the first Chinese group of importing wholesalers who attempted to adulterate heroin prior to sale. Seizures by P.R.C. officials have identified a dramatic increase in No. 4 heroin from 6.7 kilograms in 1985 to fourteen-hundred fifty kilograms in 1990.

Chinese traffickers have created new transit routes by taking advantage of the P.R.C.'s open economic and trade policies. U.S. and P.R.C. law enforcement officials estimate that an average of thirty heroin refineries exist just beyond the Yunnan Province in Myanmar's Kokang region.

The D.E.A. works closely with the P.R.C. In August, 1986, the D.E.A., the P.R.C., and Thai police seized 22 kilograms of heroin in Yunnan. In March, 1988, the D.E.A. controlled delivery of 4.5 kilograms of heroin—concealed in carp—from Shanghai to San Francisco. In the "Golden Carp" case subsequent arrests occurred in both cities. In April, 1989, the

D.E.A. controlled delivery of 40 kilograms of heroin shipped from Guangzhou to New York via Toronto. P.R.C. Customs and Police, Canadian Customs and Police, the Hong Kong Narcotics Bureau, the D.E.A. and United States Customs worked to investigate the case. The Asian Heroin Task Force located in New York, embodying seven different state, local, and federal agencies, also lent its assistance.

Long distance telephone tolls reveal an emerging geographic pattern in drug trafficking. Key message centers include New York, Taipei, Guangzhou, Hong Kong, Fuzhou, Kunming, Lashio, Mandalay, Bangkok, Singapore, and Chiang Mai. The statistical patterns make the emerging drug traffic appear boundless. International cooperation is needed among countries but may be a very difficult and painful experience which many countries may not want to address.

The United States government generally approaches drug trafficking, inter alia, by having the D.E.A. train foreign law enforcement officers and intelligence analysts in their respective countries, at regional schools, and at D.E.A.'s headquarters in Washington, D. C. The U.S. government funds various United Nations projects and encourages Interpol and the Chemical Action Task Force to examine global control of precursor chemicals. Providing assistance about drug-related health problems cited by the National Institute of Drug Abuse, the U.S. government granted D.E.A. tours of the United States to high-ranking foreign law enforcement officers to meet their American counterparts and discuss mutual problems.

Sharing case work concerning narcotics prevention provides a key towards international cooperation. D.E.A. practitioners operating outside the United States also work on drug prevention.

In the P.R.C., the D.E.A. works with enforcement officers in the Ministry of Public Security, the Ministry of Public Health, and the Customs General Administration. China's law enforcement resources and cooperative policies are also taken into account, but narcotic concerns range from the mundane to the complex, and the latter provides a learning experience as cooperation develops.

The P.R.C. and D.E.A. exchange telephone subscriber data, company and criminal records, hotel background information, and customs search requests. These basic exchanges become very important in completing the organizational puzzle of international drug trafficking.

Mutual assistance is needed to conduct both physical and technical surveillance of targets. Surveillance may be linked to additional hard intelligence such as the location of heroin labs, the movement of drug profits, the location of illegal crops, the identification of corrupt bankers and corrupt officials, and the specific location of drugs to be seized. Corroboration and confirmation of information on drugs among law enforcement agents remain essential. Feedback remains particularly crucial in evaluating the credibility of an informant in other countries.

The D.E.A. has been moving into even more complex areas of cooperation, and other countries will have to ask themselves difficult questions. Will these countries allow a defendant to travel to another country to make a final delivery, or instead make a drug seizure to boost their own record in drug prevention and thus gain publicity? Will they permit their law enforcement agents to give testimony in another country's court of law to assist in prosecuting a violator when the agents may reveal some confidential investigation methods? Do they define the guidelines for intra-country cooperation? Will they share a witnesses's testimony with another country in cases involving defendants in related cases? Will they enable a witness to travel to another country to furnish testimony?

The P.R.C.'s cooperation in the famous 1988 "Golden Carp" case marked the second time an Asian country permitted a witness to testify in another country. The witness loan program suffered a setback when a Chinese witness, in the middle of testifying in the United States, requested asylum. The incident created embarrassment for both the P.R.C. police and the D.E.A. The D.E.A. and the United States Attorney General's office agreed to doing everything possible to ensure that a loaned P.R.C. witness was returned to China.

Countries may eventually respond positively to questions of cooperation by enacting laws answering these questions. However, law enforcement agencies grapple with these questions now. When a large conspiracy case emerges, will an agency allow its defendants to be tried in another country, forfeiting publicity for its own agency? When an agency has the opportunity to arrest a major trafficker, will the agency desist, because another country advises that the trafficker may be in the middle of an international narcotics deal? Would it be better to make the arrest *after* large, major negotiations have been concluded?

These questions about cooperation are currently confronted by law enforcement practitioners. It would be prudent to try to answer these questions before they arise in an international narcotics case when time constraints compel enforcement groups to take action.

Cooperation in narcotics cases is a learning experience for the international law enforcement community. As countries work together on cases, a firm foundation, based on trust and the pursuit of a mutual goal, will be set. Certainly in drug trafficking cases, no reasonable person would question another country's motives to enforce the law.

In the fight against international drug trafficking, law enforcement agencies cannot afford to consider cases as small or simple. Agencies must strive to work together in neutralizing major trafficking organizations, because each country's citizenry expect and deserve nothing less.

The Soviet Union: Disorganization and Organized Crime [1]

by Joseph Serio

Introduction of *glasnost* into Soviet society and its subsequent movement toward a market economy have caused an unprecedented wave of economic crime. Multimillion ruble embezzlements have become commonplace. Encroachment on nascent private business to launder money has skyrocketed. Simplification of customs and border regulations are now and will continue to be exploited for criminal purposes. Legal regulation of foreign economic activity and severity of criminal punishments have fallen significantly behind the demands of reality. The result is a qualitatively higher level of organization in Soviet crime, characterized in part by its widening international scope. This paper discusses features of Soviet organized crime, challenges facing the Ministry of Internal Affairs (MVD) of the USSR, and the effect of Soviet organized crime on the international community.

General Characteristics of Soviet Oranganized Crime

Organized crime was officially recognized by the Soviet Government in the December 1989 speech of then-Minister of Internal Affairs, V.V. Bakatin (appointed head of the Committee for State Security, or KGB, in August 1991), at the Second Congress of People's Deputies.[2] It would be misleading, however, to suggest that this marked the actual birth of organized forms of crime in the country. Such crime had found expression in pre-revolutionary Russia. Current debate in the Soviet Union considers the characteristics necessary in group crime to earn the label "*organized* crime" and the origins of this phenomenon. The varying definitions and origins of "organized crime" will not be considered further here. Regardless of its origins, organized crime is a fact of Soviet life in the 1990s.

In this enormous country consisting of 15 republics that span 11 time zones[3], an estimated 4-5,000 active organized criminal groups exist according to MVD officials. The size of most groups ranges from 5 to 100 members. Some of the largest groups may have anywhere from 100-1500 people. On average, groups exist up to one-and-a-half to two years and commit 18-20 crimes.[4] Nearly a quarter of gang membership consists of students, athletes and ex-servicemen.[5]

According to the Ministry of Internal Affairs' Sixth Main Department for the Control of the Most Dangerous Crimes, Organized Crime, Corruption and Narcobusiness[6], a "criminal group is a stable, hierarchical, organized group of two or more people, having at least a two-level organizational structure of administration, created for the systematic commission of profit-oriented crime and possessing (or attempting to possess) a system of protection through the use of corruption."[7]In reality, MVD officials feel that the number of members of a criminal organization, its structure, and its corrupted or international connections are not vital in defining organized crime. There may be as few as one of the above characteristics or several, depending on the circumstances.[8]

MVD officials believe the internal structure of organized crime groups is similar to that of organized crime "families" in the United States.[9] According to Anatoli Volobuev, the general model of the organized crime community is represented by a pyramid.[10] The base is occupied by the various operatives of the underworld (burglars, con men, black marketeers) who execute orders from above.

The next layer closer to the apex is occupied by two groups: the "supply group" and the "security group". In short, among the supply group's tasks are to ensure execution of directives from the elite by the operatives at the base of the pyramid; to settle conflicts between various criminal groupings composing the system's lower echelon; to provide stable communications between the organized criminal community and other similar organizations; and to disseminate propaganda and spread its criminal ideology. The security group may include corrupt officials, journalists, physicians and those distinguished in the arts. They contribute to the higher efficiency of the organized criminal community's actions by providing social prestige to the higher echelon members; create conditions that impede efficient countermeasures against the criminal community; take measures to discharge the criminal community members from criminal responsibility, or to mitigate punishment; provide operators with false documents (i.e. medical or employment records).

The elite group carries out organizational, administrative and ideological functions. As a rule, they do not themselves commit illegal acts, and are thus beyond the reach of Soviet criminal law, which does not define planners as participants. They develop strategies and tactics of criminal activity, search for new spheres of criminal activity, and maintain control over the supply and security groups.[11]

In Russian there is a special label literally translated as "thieves in law" (*vory v zakone*) denoting the highest level of the criminal world operating over a vast area, a whole city, region, or even republic. Confidential sources close to the Soviet underworld claim there also exist *vory v ramke*, or "thieves in a frame," indicating that their operations are spread throughout the country, although there is not conclusive evidence of this. As a rule, these thieves are from dysfunctional families[12], lead spartan lives, forsaking all comforts of a "normal" existence, and spend most of their lives in prison. There, where they themselves set prison rules rather than the prison administration, *vory* orchestrate both inside and outside prison activities of many criminal groups; "import" into the prison liquor, narcotics and other forbidden items; maintain the *obshchak* (a fund to support the groups' activities, bribe officials, and care for the families of imprisoned members, for example); sustain communication with other groups; represent, when in freedom, their groups at the *skhodki*, or "meetings", with other *vory;* and carry on similar activities.[13]As of June 1991, according to MVD intelligence, there were some 700 *vory v zakone* identified in the Soviet Union, an increase of approximately 200 from the previous year.[14]

Criminal groups are named in one of three ways: according to the territory they control (for example, the group known as "Solntsevo" hails from the Solntsevo region of Moscow), according to the ethnic background of the group members (the "Chechen" organized crime group consists of ethnic Chechens from the Northern Caucasus region of the Soviet Union), or according to the name or nickname of the leader (hence, the group known as "Boris" named after its leader).[15] Spheres of influence, both by territory and by criminal specialty, are divided among groups, and armed clashes do occur when there are conflicting interests.[16] Through the end of 1990 and into 1991, several such shootouts did occur in Moscow alone in which innocent bystanders were killed and others injured. In April 1991, Moscow organized crime groups called for a "war" to expel the Chechen group from the capital. Two theories circulated the streets of Moscow to explain why the "war" did not materialize: the Chechens, the most powerful group in Moscow, either learned of the attempt beforehand and took preventive measures, or the Sixth Main Department prevented the battle from commencing. What does not seem to be in dispute, however, is that groups do actively cooperate among themselves when necessary. *Moscow News* reported, "[A]greements were sealed between criminals in different republics....Knowing that the Tver gangsters can muster two hundred armed toughs in a matter of one hour, Moscow gangs started to use their services in their feuds."[17]

Current levels of "organization" allow for the merging of activities in the criminal and economic spheres. Activities include: racketeering, fraud, theft, robbery, armed robbery, drug dealing and trafficking, weapons trade, smuggling, prostitution, gambling, profiteering, and embezzling in the economic and banking spheres. It should be noted that, as of June 1991, Soviet officials felt that organized crime had not yet developed to the point of influencing legislation considered by the Supreme Soviet.[18]

Along with the development of traditional forms of organized crime, new types of unlawful businesses have appeared. Taking advantage of loopholes in legislation, operators in the so-called "shadow economy" amass huge sums of money and entrench themselves in the domestic market, using illegal methods to extract resources, goods, and monetary instruments from the country.

For example, instead of the real value of an export shipment, a fictitious one is indicated on customs declarations, thus high quality materials are exported as "waste." Numerous attempts to export strategic raw materials as "waste" have been prevented.

As the result of a new system of quota and licensing requirements for the acquisition of raw materials on the domestic market intended for export, shipping documents passing customs checkpoints are frequently accompanied by bribes. These raw materials are then exported in exchange for Western manufactured goods which are resold at high prices on the Soviet domestic market. This is the most common type of export-import activity which attracts "shadow economy" capital.[19]

The shortage in the USSR of computer technology has given rise to a greater demand for these products both stimulating an increase of exports to the USSR, and significantly increasing the market price of computers in the USSR above average world prices. The possibility of excessive profit has attracted organized criminal groups to this business. According to MVD intelligence estimates, in Moscow alone operators have earned profits in excess of one billion rubles by dealing in computers at black market prices. This competition for marketshares is accompanied by sharp clashes between groups, resulting in a number of casualties.[20]

The Sixth Department

The Sixth Department of the MVD, based at the Ministry's headquarters on Zhitnaya Street in Moscow, is the main law enforcement organ assigned to combat organized crime in the Soviet Union.[21] Just three years ago (1988) the Soviet Union did not officially count organized crime among the long list of problems it faced. The forces unleashed by *glasnost,* however, made it impossible to avoid. The Department was created by an order (*prikaz*) issued by Minister Bakatin at the end of 1988, and became functional in January 1989. It was only at the Second Congress of People's Deputies in December of that year that the existence of organized crime was officially recognized.

The Department is small, numbering approximately 85 personnel working in four units.[22] Sixth Department chief, A.

I. Gurov, noted that the Soviet Union is just beginning to establish contacts in law enforcement circles around the world, and still lacks treaties, agreements and contacts with other countries. But he is quick to point out that progress has been made in this area, citing the Soviet Union's recent entry into Interpol, its working relationship with the United Nations and its exchange program with the Office of International Criminal Justice (OICJ) at the University of Illinois at Chicago (UIC).[23]

Problems Facing the Ministry

The problems facing the MVD are considerable. Among the most serious is a new reliance on firearms by organized crime groups, frequently better equipped than the police. To appreciate the general increase of violence in crime, including organized crime, consider the following. According to Article 218 of the 1990 Criminal Code of the Russian Soviet Federal Socialist Republic, the illegal use, manufacture, or sale of firearms is punishable by up to 5 years in prison. Despite this, the proliferation of firearms around the country has increased dramatically. A 1988 estimate put the number of unregistered guns in the USSR between 15 and 17 million.[24] Firearms are acquired in several ways. First, some of the 3.6 million hunting rifles in the hands of some 3.2 million individuals are beginning to be used in the commission of crime.[25] These arms represent a new feature of weapons proliferation in the Soviet Union.

Second, volunteer groups that are supposedly searching for and re-burying soldiers who were killed in World War II and left in mass graves are actually looking for, and finding, well-preserved weapons and ammunition.

Third, army soldiers are selling their weapons. This is particularly true of the disillusioned servicemen returning from Afghanistan. Army officers also exchange weapons for goods in short supply such as construction materials.

Fourth, there is an active black market in arms, some of which come from abroad. Stories have appeared in the Soviet press publicizing price lists of all types of weapons available on the black market, ranging from the 25 year old Makarov pistol used by the Ministry of Internal Affairs going for 1,500 rubles, all the way to army tanks for $10,000 in United States currency.[26]

Finally, weapons are stolen from the plants that produce them, from army and police arsenals, and from trains carrying military equipment.[27]

Current Soviet criminal legislation does not provide a specific definition of "organized crime" and, perhaps more importantly, does not provide sanctions for the creation of a criminal organization in its contemporary meaning. It allows only for the prosecution of individual members of these groups for participating in crime. Members of organized groups are prosecuted most often for smuggling, embezzlement of state property, extortion, fraud, profiteering, robbery, armed robbery, premeditated murder, serious bodily injury, as well as drug-related crime.[28] The length of imprisonment ranges from 5 to 15 years. As one MVD official complains, the Criminal Code "envisages no punishment of those criminal bosses who provide all the logistics for the criminal businesses but who haven't committed any concrete crimes."[29]

Sanctions for "money laundering" are not provided for by law, allowing an increase in the number of illegal transactions, which inflicts serious damage on the economy of the country. It is widely believed that so-called "cooperative" restaurants, cafes and other establishments (essentially private businesses) springing up in the Soviet Union are actively exploited to launder money. A 1989 estimate revealed that "1 out of the [then] 512 'top-category' thieves (i.e. *vory v zakone*) in the country is a member of a cooperative."[30]

There are provisions for the confiscation of property. According to Article 35 of the Criminal Code of the Russian

Federation published in 1990 and accompanying commentary, confiscation "pertains only to personal property of the accused and his portion of common property. Property needed by those in the accused's care...is excluded".[31] Property seized, however, such as computers, automobiles, and monetary instruments, is not directed back to law enforcement organs to help support their work.[32] Article 35 does not contain special provisions regarding property acquired through organized criminal activity.

Regarding witness protection, the law requires the police, investigator, procurator, and the court to adopt measures to protect the life and property of victims, witnesses or other participants in a case, as well as the members of their families or close relatives when sufficient evidence exists that they are threatened by murder, violence, destruction or damage to property.[33] In reality, the resources needed to implement these provisions are not available. Indeed, police occasionally lack vehicles to transport witnesses to court.[34] In addition, protective measures are not extended to informants and other participants in the trial procedure, as witnesses, names and addresses are listed on the last page of the indictment.[35]

At present, the Sixth Department is studying the American experience in fighting organized crime, particularly the Racketeer Influenced and Corrupt Organizations (RICO) law to assist in devising a comprehensive legislative base through which to launch a more serious effort against organized crime.

A series of organizational and administrative problems also hampers the Sixth Department in its effort to control organized crime. The entrenched political structure of the Soviet Union has proven a formidable hindrance in pursuing cases against organized crime groups and those associated with these groups, such as corrupt State officials, including employees of the Ministry itself. Employees of local ministries of internal affairs are subordinate not only to the All-Union Ministry in Moscow but also to local political bodies. Ministry leaders at the local level frequently develop close relations with the local political leaders. Hence, investigations are frequently stalled, sabotaged, or simply shelved.[36]

Lack of coordination negatively affects the Ministry's work. The task of coordinating the activities of the various MVD departments falls on the seven deputy ministers. For example, one deputy minister is assigned to coordinate activities among the Sixth Department, the Criminal Investigation Department, and BKhSS—the so-called Economic Police which combats theft of state property and profiteering activities. In the first five months of 1991, there were three different deputy ministers occupying this post, only one of whom was a professional law enforcement officer. He was at the helm less than two weeks before being transferred to another position. When deputy ministers do serve in these posts for some time there are complaints that their guidance is inadequate since they usually do not grasp the essence of the law enforcement problem. Currently (June 1991) only one of the seven deputy ministers has spent his professional life in law enforcement. The others for the most part were chosen from the *nomenklatura*, that list of elite Communist Party officials who are selected for the most prestigious posts in government.

Lack of technology also presents serious problems. Everything from handcuffs and guns to electronic surveillance devices and even cars are in short supply, forcing the police to turn frequently to the KGB for technical assistance. This clouds the division of labor between the two agencies, a perennial problem in the Soviet Union.

As a result of incompetence at high levels in the Ministry, bureaucratic infighting, lack of technology, as well as low pay[37], many highly qualified law enforcement officers are attracted to the developing private sector, finding financially beneficial positions as security personnel in joint ventures, commercial banks, and other enterprises. Addressing these problems is necessary if the USSR wishes to make serious inroads on organized crime.

Effects on the International Community

One effect of the overall worsening of crime prevention in the USSR is the inability of law enforcement bodies to ensure the safety of foreigners. In 1990 nearly 8,000 crimes against foreigners were registered, of which 64 percent were thefts of personal property and 13 percent were robberies. Whereas previously foreigners were off-limits to the criminal world, they are now actively targetted by organized crime groups: credit card rings, taxi cab service rings, and prostitution rings, among others. Businessmen in particular are targetted.

In addition, companies that have successfully established themselves in the Soviet Union suffer losses due to fraud. They unwittingly become involved in export-import deals with unscrupulous Soviet partners, often suffering monetary losses as well as loss in prestige.

These activities are not restricted to the Soviet Union. As border restrictions ease, a tremendous international increase in these activities will occur. Indeed, Soviet organized crime groups already actively smuggle stolen automobiles from Europe, particularly from Germany, into the Soviet Union.[38] They are involved in fraudulent activities in computer sales with major operations already established in Poland, Bulgaria, Czechoslovakia, and other East European countries, as well as in the United States. The Chechen group mentioned earlier is already operating as far west as Austria, and other groups actively work in Germany.[39]

The New York City neighborhood of Brighton Beach is well known as a large Soviet emigre community as well as fertile ground for Soviet organized crime in America. In addition, there is a large Armenian population in Los Angeles that is also beginning to flex its muscle in the criminal world. For example, a crime figure convicted of credit card fraud is reputed to have amassed a fortune of more than $600 million from bootlegged gasoline in less than a decade after his arrival in the US. Illegal emigre activities range from "old-fashioned jewelry swindles" to multi-million-dollar schemes involving fake credit cards and bootlegged gasoline. To complicate matters, there are reports that Soviet organized groups have already begun working in conjunction with the New York crime "families."[40]

As Aeroflot, the Soviet airline, increases direct flights from the USSR to the United States, and immigration increases dramatically in 1993 after the implementation of the new Soviet immigration law, there is expected to be a significant increase of Soviet crime in America. Indeed, law enforcement agencies predict that a wave of Soviet crime will sweep across Europe and America within five years. Many of these crimes will be committed by organized groups, some of whom will develop criminal networks all over the world.

It will be exceedingly difficult for law enforcement agencies around the world to deal with Soviet organized crime for several reasons. Soviet criminals have been subjected to severe conditions under imprisonment in their country, and will consider Western prisons slight punishment for their crimes. They also are highly secretive and their networks will prove difficult to infiltrate.   An ever-present obstacle is finding enough law enforcement officers proficient in the various languages of the Soviet Union; a Russian-speaking police officer will be useless against a gang from Armenia or Georgia.

Soviet organized crime clearly presents a major problem to many countries of the world and will challenge law enforcement for years to come. It is imperative to understand the problem now and begin to stem the tide.

Notes

1. This presentation is based on research and observations done during the author's nine-month internship at the Sixth Department for Organized Crime Control, Ministry of InternalAffairs, USSR, September 1990 - June 1991.

2. See the subsequently adopted Decision of the Congress of People's Deputies of the Union of Soviet Socialist Republics, *Ob usilenii bor'by s organizovannoi prestupnost'iu (On strengthening the fight against organized crime)* signed by President Gorbachev, 23 December 1989, in Appendix to A.I. Gurov, *Professional'naia Prestupnost' (Professional Crime)* (1990).

3. This presentation was given before the failed coup of August 1991. The author would contend that, in spite of the transformation and partial break-up of the Soviet Union, organized crime will continue to grow at a rapid pace.

4. Author interview with A.I. Gurov, head of the Sixth Department, 25 April 1991. It should be noted that statistics regarding Soviet organized crime are only rough estimates. According to one of the Soviet pioneers in the academic study of organized crime, there has been no reliable method to count the numbers of groups, group members, or weapons.

5. L. Fisher, "Gangsters of the New Generation," *Sovetskaia Militsiia* 4 (1991): 2-5, interview with militia colonel Valeri Pakhomov.

6. The "Sixth Department for Organized Crime Control" was upgraded to the "Sixth Main Department for Combatting the Most Serious Forms of Crime, Organized Crime, Corruption and Narcobusiness" by Presidential Decree of 4 February 1991, entitled "On measures to strengthen the fight against the most serious crimes and their organized forms" ("O merakh po usileniiu bor'by s naibolee opasnymi prestupleniiami i ikh organizovannymi formami"). The "Sixth Department" is one of three numbered departments in the MVD. The others are the "Seventh" and "Eighth". Most departments, such as Criminal Investigation, are not denoted by number.

7. Organized Crime Survey Response, MVD, USSR. The Survey Response was an internal document prepared by the leadership of the Sixth Department and translated by the author of this paper in preparation for a United Nations-MVD Conference on Organized Crime Control held in the USSR from 21-25 October 1991.

8. *Ibid.*

9. Author interview with G.F. Chebotarev, deputy head of Sixth Department, 7 February 1991.

10. For an illustration of the pyramid, see Anatoli Volobuev, "Combatting Organized Crime in the USSR: Problems and Perspectives," *CJ International*, 5, no. 6: 13.

11. see Anatoli Volobuev, "Combatting Organized Crime in the USSR: Problems and Perspectives," in *International Perspectives on Organized Crime*, ed. Jane Rae Buckwalter (Chicago: Office of International Criminal Justice, 1990): 75-82; and A.N. Volobuev in *Organizovannaia Prestupnost'*, ed. A.I. Dolgova (1989): 28-42.

12. One frequently occurring characteristic of those who become thieves is a fatherless childhood, and is illustrated in the following verses from a thieves' song: "And so, without a father to support me/I left my home and went into the streets/A path that soon would lead me straight to prison/Branded with the name, and fate, of thief", in Mikhail Dyomin, *The Day is Born of Darkness* (New York: Alfred A. Knopf, 1976), 55.

13. For a full discussion of the customs and traditions of *vory v zakone*, see *Osobo Opasnie Lidery v ITU i Vospitatel'noe Vozdeistvie Na Nikh*, *(Particularly Dangerous Leaders in Prison and How to Reform Them)*, ed. Iu. M. Antonian (Moscow: All-Union Scientific Research Institute, 1989).

14. Gennady Chebotarev, "Organized Crime in an International Dimension" in *International Perspectives on Organized Crime*, ed. Jane Rae Buckwalter (Chicago: Office of International Criminal Justice, 1990): 95.

15. Author interview with Chebotarev, 17 January 1991.

16. See "Moskovskii reket: Khotiat li gangstery voiny?" ("The Moscow Racket: Do the Gangsters Want War?") *Kommersant* 46 (26 November-3 December 1990): 24-25.

17. "'Godfathers' End Up in a Clink", no. 19: 15.

18. Author interview with G. F. Chebotarev, 4 May 1991.

19. See paper by G.F. Chebotarev, "Organized Crime in Export-Import Operations", presented at the 20th European Regional Conference of Interpol (London, 3-5 April 1991).

20. *Ibid.*

21. The MVD's Sixth Department is joined by the KGB and the Procurator's office in fighting organized crime. This section deals only with the MVD since the Sixth Department has taken the lead role in fighting organized crime, many of the scientists to first research this problem a decade ago come from the MVD, the Sixth Department is fairly visible in Soviet society, and the author's access was greatest to the Sixth Department.

22. Since this writing, the department has expanded to some 200 personnel, has received funding for purchasing technology, and has formed a unit to fight terrorism.

23. See Joseph Serio, "The Sixth Department: Fighting Organized Crime in the Soviet Union", *CJ International* 7, no. 3: 8-9.

24. *Kazakhstanskaia Pravda* 24 as cited in Aaron Trehub, "Privately Owned Weapons in the Soviet Union", *Radio Free Europe/Radio Free Liberty*, 5 December 1988. Other estimates vary. According to reports in the American press, Soviet press estimates of the number of weapons in private hands range from 50,000 to 500,000. See Bill Keller, "Soviet Black Market In Weapons Spreads" *San Francisco Chronicle*, 9 November 1990; "[L]aw enforcement authorities in Moscow estimate that Soviets have 3.6 million illegal guns," in "Soviets illegally armed 'to the teeth'" *San Jose Mercury News* 11 December 1990. According to comments by G. F. Chebotarev at the OICJ Sixth Annual International Symposium on Criminal Justice Issues (22 August 1991), 14,000 firearms are now officially wanted by police.

25. These are official Soviet figures cited in Graham H. Turbiville, Jr. and James F. Gebhardt, "Soviet Union: The Enemies Within" (Fort Leavenworth, Kansas: Foreign Military Studies Office, US Army,: 4. This was a reprint from the article originally published in Army (April 1991): 30-41.

26. "What are we buying weapons for?" *Komsomol' skaia Pravda* 6 (November 1990): 1.

27. Turbiville and Gebhardt, *op.cit.* note 25: 5.

28. Survey Response.

29. Fisher, *op.cit.* note 5.

30. A. Sergeyev and A. Shulus, "The Working People and the Shadow Economy: Who Will Win?" *Literaturnaia Rossiia* 2 (1990): 2-4.

31. *Kommentarii k Ugolovnomu Kodeksu RSFSR, (Commentary to the Criminal Code of the RSFSR)* (1984): 78. See also *Ugolovnyi Kodeks RSFSR (Criminal Code of the RSFSR)* Article 35 (1990): 27-28. Although the Criminal Code was published in 1990 and the Commentary in 1984 from the previous Criminal Code, there were no changes in the specific provisions considered here over the six-year period.

32. Author interview with A. I. Gurov, 25 April 1991; See also Gurov interview with Yuri Shchekochikhin, "Hunting the Lion," *Literaturnaia Gazeta* 21 (1990): 12.

33. Survey Response. See also Soviet law passed by the Supreme Soviet of the USSR on 12 May 1990, "O vnesenii izmenenii i dopolnenii v Osnovi ugolovnogo sudoproizvodstva Soiuza SSR i soiuznikh respublik" ("On changes and supplements to the Fundamentals of legal proceedings of the USSR and the Union Republics).

34. "Godfathers...", *op.cit.* note 17.

35. *Ibid.*

36. Recent developments in the Soviet Union, including the fall of the Communist Party, give hope that this system will be changed in the near future.

37. In 1991, one of the deputy heads of the Sixth Department accepted a position with the Organized Crime Control Department of the Russian Republic MVD because of favorable salary.

38. This is based on Sixth Department information. For an account of Soviet organized crime activities in Germany, see Marc Pitzke, "Soviet Mafia Terrorise Jewish Immigrant Businesses in Berlin" *Reuter News Service*, 19 September 1991.

39. Sixth Department information.

40. For accounts of Soviet criminal involvement in New York and Los Angeles, see Yuri Shchekochikhin, "'Nashi' v Amerike" ("'Ours' in America"), *Literaturnaia Gazeta*, no. 18: 8; James Rosenthal, "Russia's New Export: The Mob", *Washington Post*, 24 June 1990, sec. 3; Ralph Blumenthal with Celestine Bohlen, "Soviet Emigre Mob Outgrows Brooklyn, and Fear Spreads", *New York Times*, 4 June 1989, sec. 1; Tim Cornwell, "Soviet Mafia Moves West", *The European*, 30 August - 1 September 1991; Ronald L. Soble, "Moscow Writer Searches for Soviet No-Goodniks in L.A.", *Los Angeles Times*, 2 March 1991, sec. B.

Index

U

V

W